Phyllis Schlafly Speaks, Volume 4

Patents and Invention

Phyllis Schlafly

Edited by Ed Martin

Permission to quote in critical reviews with citation:
Patents and Invention
By Phyllis Schlafly

ISBN 978-0-9984000-9-9

Skellig
AMERICA

TABLE OF CONTENTS

This book is dedicated to

John G. Trump (1907-1985)

Uncle of President Donald J. Trump

&

John B. "Bruce" Stewart (1878-1955)

Father of Phyllis Schlafly

Whose lives of invention and patent-holding inspired

Donald J. Trump and Phyllis Schlafly

to work for American exceptionalism and the U.S. Constitution

Editor's Note by Ed Martin

T he fourth-grade teacher assigned her pupils the assignment: bring a paragraph of writing *each day*. More than 70 years later, in an interview for the Abraham Lincoln's Presidential Library's Illinois Statecraft *Oral History* project, Phyllis Schlafly would recall it as the beginning of her lifelong habit of writing. This habit generated thousands of daily columns and daily radio commentaries, almost 50 books (in part or whole), and almost uncountable letters and speeches.

Around the time she began these paragraph-a-day assignments, Phyllis watched her father, John B. Schlafly, each evening after supper. Her father, who had lost his good job as a sales engineer at Westinghouse Company in the Depression and worked a succession of lesser jobs, went to his workbench most evenings to work on a rotary engine that might just work better than existing ones. He was a dogged worker, an inventor, and he received a patent on his rotary engine.

The Schlafly engine did not bring fame or fortune but it remained in Phyllis' memory. Later, when she was well-established as one of America's great leaders and a foremost expert on the U.S. Constitution, she would conclude that the American inventiveness and our patent system was a singular achievement in human history. In the preceding years, as this volume of her writing shows, she thought through this history and America's place in it. Now knowing her story, it's hard to read the words without recognizing a daughter's esteem for her inventive father.

The *Phyllis Schlafly Speaks* series collects Phyllis' writings by topic and field of interest. It is, as the saying goes, only the tip of the iceberg. More volumes to follow: after all, those paragraphs each day adds up fast!

Foreword by Charles Schott

P hyllis Schlafly (1924-2016) was an important American grassroots activist and public intellectual who engaged in advocacy on a broad range of public issues. Her *New York Times* obituary noted that "(h)er energy was formidable. She wrote or edited more than 20 books, published an influential monthly newsletter beginning in 1967, appeared daily on nearly 500 radio stations and delivered regular commentaries on CBS television in the 1970s and CNN in the '80s."

She was known for her "conservative activism" on important issues, such as opposition to the dangers posed to the U.S. by international communism, the fight for women's rights outside the confines of the proposed Equal Rights Amendment (ERA) and also on a broad range of policy and procedural issues within the Republican party. It was in the Republican party where she served as a national convention Platform Committee member and as part of the leadership of the National Federation of Republican Women.

Phyllis Schlafly engaged on a broad range of issues that did not just include family-related matters, such as the importance of traditional marriage, but also on a broad array of economic, trade, education, national defense and international issues.

Her areas of interest (and associated areas of impact) were broader than her image often conveyed. These different areas could almost always be characterized as containing a general theme about the importance of fighting for the interests of the average citizen (i.e., "the little guy") in the face of the invariable behind the scenes efforts of governments, large corporations, internationalists and establishment elites (particularly those found on the U. S. east and west coasts).

In addition to these other areas of policy interest, however, Phyllis Schlafly had a strong and enduring interest in issues relating to invention, patents and other forms of intellectual property (including copyrights). These intellectual property and innovation issues were very important to her and fundamentally underpinned her views on why America was a great, successful (and unique) country.

The importance of the American system of patents and invention was a theme that she returned to again and again over the years (as you can see from the dates associated with the different articles included in this volume).

Phyllis Schlafly cared about these invention, patent and intellectual property issues for a number of important reasons. Patents and invention were central to the founding of the United States and to its enduring prosperity. The rights of the average person to obtain a patent or copyright to protect his or her inventive work were contained in the body of the original Constitution. They were the only rights set forth in the original Constitution prior to the addition of the Bill of Rights. These rights to defend the value of one's inventive work product are fundamental rights, similar to the right a laborer has to the benefits of his or her own labor.

The patent system as authorized by the Constitution was both new and uniquely American, based in the creation of a property right in one's own inventions. She was known to say that it both helped explain why 95% of all inventions were developed in the United States and the origins of America's prosperity. It wasn't just the presence of abundant natural resources, as other countries were similarly endowed without having the productivity and creativity that our patent system unleashed.

Importantly, she often noted how this economic dynamism continues to characterize the U.S. economy *vis-a-vis* the rest of the world. She was able to point to numerous examples of where the American system of encouraging invention and patents had created "an explosion of human energy, an expansion of wealth, a rise in living standards that exceeded all the economic changes in the thousands of years that preceded our Constitution."

She could also point to familiar names of important inventors in such fields as communications (Samuel Morse, Thomas Edison and Alexander Graham Bell, among others), transportation (Henry Ford, Orville and Wilbur Wright, et al.), industry and energy (Captain James Eads and the DuPont family) whose inventions transformed America and the world.

She often returned to Thomas Jefferson's comment that "(t)he issue of patents for new discoveries has given a spring to invention beyond my conception." Jefferson had been the first administrator of the American Patent System. President Lincoln had been an inventor and patent holder before being elected.

Phyllis Schlafly recognized that many of the matters raised concerning patents and copyright were fundamental and represented important Constitutional issues. This theme recurs time and again in her writings, involving such areas as the constitutional primacy of "first-to-invent" over "first-to-file," due process claims concerning proposed new administrative post-grant reviews of patents (after they have been awarded), and also when a proposed change in existing patent rights might constitute an improper Constitutional "taking."

She pointed out how inventors had been (and continued to be) the "liberators" of women throughout American history. In 1970, Phyllis published an important article by Vicki Rutledge in *The Phyllis Schlafly Report* called, "You've Come A Long Way Baby, But Who Gave You A Lift?" The article pays tribute to the many inventors (many of them men) whose inventions "have liberated women from the once all time-consuming drudgery of housework. Because of their help, women today have time to fulfill their own ambitions ..."

The policy issues associated with invention and patents were also a key battlefield in the fight between the rights of the average citizen and the large economic entities who could play the game in secret and behind the scenes. It was always presented as an important area where sunlight and logical argument could serve as an important public disinfectant whenever "the fix was in!"

These issues arose in various settings, such as in the attempt to transform the Patent Trademark Office (PTO) into a private corporation (with an "advisory" board of directors consisting mostly of big company executives) and the diversion of PTO filing fees to other non-patent purposes by the Congress. Phyllis Schlafly recognized the truth in the old libertarian adage that "no person's life and property are truly safe so long as the Legislature is in session."

Phyllis Schlafly also recognized the importance of the international dimension of invention, patent and other intellectual property issues. Other nations did not have patent regimes until the United States' example showed them the way (and the benefits). Even so, she often pointed out how foreign patent regimes tend to be designed to benefit large companies and the elites in other societies. Often, these other countries' interest in the U.S. patent system has been to make it easier for them to appropriate (she would say "steal") the secrets of American inventors. "Foreign countries are free to copy our system," she wrote. "Instead they want to copy our inventions." The "secret deal" made between Commerce Secretary Ron

Brown and Japan concerning various issues of so-called "patent reform" is one such example. China's largely successful effort to improperly take American intellectual property in connection with its "indigenous innovation" policy is another.

Phyllis Schlafly will be remembered for her constant vigilance against efforts aimed at the "harmonization" of the U.S. patent system with other systems internationally. She would write that all such efforts were aimed at making the U.S. system more inferior (as they sought to make the U.S. system more like other countries' systems around the world). She was clear that she would not object to efforts aimed at the "harmonization" of the rest of the world to make their patent systems more like the superior U.S. one.

She recognized the importance of mobilizing the opposition to so-called "patent reform" efforts, that she referred to as "no reform at all," but rather "a direct attack on the unique, successful American patent system created by the U.S. Constitution." This was done by mobilizing the grass-roots organizations she had founded to engage in letter and editorial writing and in contacting members of Congress. The letter written against the patent reform bill in 1997 by 26 Nobel

Prize Laureates is an excellent example of this. These internationally renowned, individually recognized experts made the point that the patent "reform" bill being considered "could result in lasting harm to the United States and the world." They observed how the unique American patent system is "a delicate structure," which "should not be subject to frequent modifications."

She also saw the important "national security" dimension of invention and patent issues. She noted how proposed patent "reform" threatens individual and corporate research and development, which is the "backbone of our national defense and economic security" in the U.S. This was seen as particularly true *vis-a-vis* the efforts to change the U.S. from a "first-to-invent" to a "first-to-file" system, which "will enable Chinese hackers to steal U.S. innovation secrets while they are in development, then file an application with the U.S. Patent Office under First-to-File, and thereby own new U.S. technology instead of merely stealing it."

It is important to recognize that these issues were also personal to Phyllis Schlafly. Her father had been an inventor and had to fight to obtain the patent he received for his invention (see Appendix 3). Patent rights had been at the foundation of Phyllis Schlafly's family history and it was something important that she took with her from growing up. "I have been interested in inventions and patents all my life. I had a father who worked many years to get a patent and he did, and likewise for a son, and, they didn't sell them, and they didn't make any money and they didn't change the world, but at any rate they were very proud of them and they were theirs. And no one can take them away from them, because of our wonderful system."

The above points were ones that Phyllis Schlafly returned to over and over again!

The important role of the inventor in the American economy also represents the area where Phyllis Schlafly connects with the dynamic, innovative and uniquely American high-tech world of Silicon Valley and the venture capital (VC) industry. It is the role of the entrepreneur and the high-tech VC industry associated with Silicon Valley, their important and unique role creating competitive new companies from forward thinking yet practical "ideas on a sheet of paper," to turn ideas into tangible business entities operating at the rate of hundreds of millions of dollars in sales (sometimes in less than a single year). The Silicon Valley start-up company's natural targets are the large established companies in the U.S. and world economies; large established incumbent companies with their own goals to use patents primarily (1) to "stave off upstarts" and (2) to control the pace of industry change and development (so as to allow for the gradual and predictable harvesting of the value of their existing business franchises).

In this regard, it has been interesting over time to watch as the VC industry's view of patents has changed. In earlier days, venture capitalists (VCs) often viewed patents as an area not worth the investment of scarce resources in a fast-changing market (e.g., "would you rather invest $30K in obtaining a patent that you will then have to pay lawyers to enforce or would you rather hire another marketing person to help in executing the business plan now?").

More recently, the VC view of patents has become one where patent assets are viewed as extremely important to a start-up company's competitive future (and, on the other side of the coin, they have been recognized as perhaps the only start-up assets with any tangible value in bankruptcy or recapitalization, thus allowing the VCs to recapture some or all of their original investment in the significant numbers of portfolio companies that do inevitably fail).

It should be mentioned that this view can reasonably be expected to change in the companies that become successful, as VC-backed "insurgent" companies become mature and traditionally successful public companies; i.e. when they become the "incumbents" in their respective markets.

It will surprise some readers how Phyllis Schlafly's philosophical "conservatism" in this area fits so well with the priorities of the most economically dynamic Silicon Valley entrepreneurs and the early stage venture capitalists who back them.

This volume is intended to help begin a process of appreciation in this area. It also represents another chance to appreciate the full extent of Phyllis Schlafly's multi-faceted legacy and the debt Americans owe to her for "a public life well lived" in the context of her important work upholding the core values and traditions of this country.

Charles Schott is a management consultant and serves as a Senior Advisor for the Center for Financial Stability (www.centerforfinancialstability.org), a New York based public policy think tank. Mr. Schott served as Deputy Assistant Secretary for Trade and Investment Policy at the U.S.

Treasury, where he was responsible for trade negotiations and for matters relating to international investment. His office was active on issues relating to the World Trade Organization and the negotiation of bilateral and regional free trade agreements, particularly on matters relating to financial services and investment. Mr. Schott also served as Chief of Staff at the U.S. Federal Communications Commission and as Deputy Assistant Secretary of Commerce and Deputy Administrator of the National Telecommunications and Information Administration (NTIA). In the private sector, Mr. Schott worked as a management consultant in the London, UK offices of McKinsey & Company, as a founding executive of Hearst New Media & Technology (an operating group of the Hearst Corporation) and Paradigm Partners, LLC, and as the head of strategic sales and marketing for Intellectual Ventures in Bellevue, WA. Intellectual Ventures is a private company that centers on the development and licensing of intellectual property and, as of 2011, was one of the top-five owners of U.S. patents.

Introduction by Phyllis Schlafly
April 6, 2011

I have been interested in inventions and patents all my life. I had a father who worked many years to get a patent and he did, and likewise for a son, and, they didn't sell them, and they didn't make any money and they didn't change the world, but at any rate they were very proud of them and they were theirs. And nobody can take them away from them, because of our wonderful system. And it was a pleasure when I was on the Bicentennial Commission by Reagan appointment to put on a really beautiful tribute to the whole idea of American inventors, and the unique system we have in this country.

It is unique. The Founding Fathers, meeting in Philadelphia, took one afternoon off from their non-air-conditioned room in Independence Hall, and went out to see that new-fangled invention, the steamboat. And they were impressed with that. And they knew that it was important, and I like to tell all of my evangelical supporters that the Founding

Fathers put and guaranteed the right of inventors to his own private property even before they put in freedom of religion and freedom of speech. It really is a remarkable thing. Prior to the Constitution, the king doled it out to his pals, and under this new system I guess we would have Obama giving out, doling out favors to his friends. But that isn't what we want. We want the individual inventor to be able to own his creation. And that's what's made our country great. And when our Founding Fathers started out, America's living conditions were pretty much like what they had been like for thousands of years. They tilled the ground the way they tilled the ground in biblical days. The women, after they slaved all day, at night they would sit at their spinning wheel. I have an antique spinning wheel, so I can tell my visitors when I've finished saving the world through the day, I can sit at my spinning wheel and weave some cloth. But fortunately, we had inventions like the sewing machine and others that relieved women from that.

And of course, at the time when our country was founded, the fastest way to get a message somewhere was to put Paul Revere on a horse and have him carry the message. And now we have all these wonderful ways—we had the telegraph, then we had the telephone, then we had the transistor, and we have the computer, and it's just simply wonderful. And the changes, the explosions of wealth and standard of living in such a few years in this country is just absolutely remarkable. And I think it is due primarily to our unique patent system. And no other country has it. It is still unique in the world. I hope you will make it your vision to nail all the Congressmen you know and tell them what's what about patents.

Chapter 1
America: Land of Opportunity
March 1970

On February 22, 1970, Phyllis Schlafly was awarded the George Washington Honor Medal by the Freedoms Foundation of Valley Forge for a speech she gave entitled, "America: Land of Opportunity," which was an address of welcome to the new citizens received at the Naturalization Ceremonies for the Eastern District of Missouri at the Federal Building in St. Louis, August 1, 1969. The George Washington Honor Medal is given for "an outstanding accomplishment in helping to achieve a better understanding of the American Way of Life."

This is that award-winning speech.

It is an honor for me to welcome such an impressive group of new American citizens.

You should be especially pleased to receive your American citizenship in St. Louis, the heart of America. At the confluence of the Mississippi and Missouri Rivers, St. Louis is one of the famous crossroads of the world. Here in this immensely fertile valley, you become a part of a nation where there are good people who will warmly welcome you to your adopted country.

We have all read much about the recent walk on the moon by the American astronauts, and of what a magnificent achievement it was. You should also know, if you do not, that St. Louis was the launching pad for two past expeditions which were comparable in importance with the recent flight to the moon. The other two expeditions took just as much courage, just as much careful planning, just as much skill on the part of its leaders. They were fraught with just as many hazards, as men set out to conquer the unknown. Both of these past expeditions were started here in St. Louis—financed by individuals who had the foresight and the courage to embark upon a dangerous journey.

The first was the Lewis and Clark expedition, one of the most important explorations in the history of the world. Commanding a team of 40 men, Meriwether Lewis and William Clark set forth from St. Louis on a frightening trip in 1804, went north by boat and on foot, and then west into territory which had never before been explored, all the way to the Pacific Ocean and what is now the State of Washington. The round trip took two years and constituted the physical taking possession by Americans of the huge western half of the United States. This is the real reason why the giant Arch proclaims St. Louis as the Gateway to the West.

The other historic expedition which started in St. Louis was Charles Lindbergh's solo flight from New York to Paris in 1927, the fabulous achievement which made him one of America's great heroes. He was able to make that trip only because farsighted businessmen in St. Louis believed in him and in the future of flying and raised the money to finance his flight. This is why Lindbergh's plane was named "The Spirit of St. Louis."

This is the kind of spirit which made America great. The initiative, the courage, the perseverance, and the determination to brave every hardship to achieve a good objective. These are the kind of men who made America the land of the free and the home of the brave.

But enough of local history. Today you become citizens of the United States of America, the great country which stretches from coast to coast, which has every kind of climate, every kind of geography, every kind of people, a land of infinite variety.

Why is it that Americans have enjoyed more material benefits than any other nation in the history of civilization? It is not because Americans are smarter than other peoples of the world. It is not because we work longer hours. It is not because our land is superior in natural resources. Russia, China, Canada and Brazil are all larger than continental United States.

No, the reason for our unique prosperity and abundance is because our Founding Fathers, the men who wrote our Constitution, gave us a system of Government which made this a land of freedom and opportunity—and this magic formula unleashed the ingenuity and resourcefulness of man.

Crude oil oozed from the ground for thousands of years and people wondered what it was good for—until American inventive genius made it the indispensable servant of modern civilization to run our automobiles, our trains, our tractors, our planes. Torrents of water rushed over Niagara Falls for untold centuries—until American genius harnessed that energy to light the darkness of night and turn the wheels of industry.

America has been able to give more good things to more people than any nation in the history of the world—NOT because Government solved our problems—but because Government stayed out of the way and let the initiative and inventiveness of man solve our problems ourselves.

On this auspicious occasion today, the best thing I can say to you is—Welcome to America, the land of opportunity, a country where there is no ceiling and there are no restrictions on the heights to which you may climb if you are willing to invest your talents and your energy.

Last year it was my privilege to conduct a national essay contest in the schools on the subject "An American Inventor." Reading many of the 60,000 essays which were submitted gave me a real appreciation of what is so great about America. The true stories of American inventors teach two principal lessons: (1) the virtues of hard work and determination in the face of tremendous odds, and (2) the fact that our high standard of living is the direct result of what we call "the American way of life," a unique political and economic system which has encouraged inventors and producers. Most American inventors had to overcome the handicap of a humble start in life or other obstacles. They achieved their goal because of the freedom and opportunity we enjoy in the United States.

Many essays, of course, were written about Thomas Edison, the greatest of American inventors, and most told of his famous statement: "The secret of what people choose to call my genius is 2% inspiration and 98% perspiration." Despite hundreds of failures, he never allowed himself to become discouraged. Try to imagine what life would be like without the electric light bulb and electric generating plants, and then you will have a measure of his gift to the world.

George Westinghouse, the inventor of the air brake which contributed so much to the safety of our railroads, started working at 5c per hour and collapsed many times from overwork, but he proved that a man can achieve any height if he really wants to in this great country of ours.

One essay told the story of the inventor of the frozen foods we enjoy today, Clarence Birdseye, who started life in poverty as the son of immigrant parents and was able because of American freedom to rise to success and wealth. The student concluded: "What made Clarence Birdseye want to make new inventions? This can be answered by the one word, freedom."

Another essay told how Walt Disney, the inventor of the animated cartoon, succeeded because he had "ideas, ideals and freedom to make his dreams come true."

Only in America could Henry Ford have invented mass manufacturing processes that gave jobs to so many Americans and enabled them all to own automobiles.

The winning essay was written by a student who told the stirring story of George Washington Carver, the Negro inventor who gave us 118 products from the sweet potato and 300 from the peanut. The essay concluded: "Where but in America could a sickly boy born of slave parents rise to such heights of scientific accomplishments? George Washington Carver was fortunate indeed to live in America, ... Doors of opportunity still swing wide in our country. But we must have initiative and ambition to pass through those doors." Carver succeeded because of his "willingness to pay the price of success"—hard work, rugged determination, and a dedication to the principles of service.

Some of you may be thinking that the United States already has 200,000,000 people, and the new citizen today is starting with a handicap that he can never overcome. Don't you believe it. The horizons are just as wide today as ever before for those who become Americans by choice instead of by the accident of birth. There is an endless roll of immigrants in our

time who have scaled the heights in every field of endeavor—
and they have received the highest rewards for their work.

President Richard Nixon's top adviser on foreign policy
and security is Henry Kissinger, an immigrant from Germany
who has been a naturalized citizen only since 1943. That such a
recent immigrant could rise to such a sensitive and powerful
position in our Government is stunning proof that America is
truly the land of opportunity for everyone.

Enrico Fermi, an immigrant from Italy, came to the
University of Chicago and led the work on the first atomic
chain reaction. In 1954, our Government awarded him a special
prize of $25,000 in recognition of his most important work in
the development of the atomic bomb.

Edward Teller, the outstanding American atomic
scientist today, is an immigrant from Hungary. He also has
been highly decorated by our Government for his contributions
to physics and to national security.

The popular composer Irving Berlin came to America
as an immigrant from Russia. He attended school for only two
years and had no formal musical education. He sold
newspapers on the Lower East Side of New York City, sang on
street corners, and was a singing waiter in Chinatown. He

probably made more money than any composer in history. Most people will say that he deserved it, but only in America could be have received it. He not only composed hundreds of popular songs, but he gave us one of our favorite Christmas carols, "White Christmas," and one of our favorite patriotic songs, "God Bless America," for which the U.S. Congress honored him with a gold medal.

The most famous of all American football coaches, Knute Rockne, was an immigrant from Norway. As the head football coach at Notre Dame University for nearly 15 years, he won lasting fame for his winning teams, for his insistence on good sportsmanship, and for his clever football strategy. His football teams won 105 games, tied 5, and lost only 12.

Everyone knows that the telephone is a great American invention. We should also remember that the inventor of the telephone, Alexander Graham Bell, was an immigrant from Scotland.

Nikola Tesla, born in what is now Yugoslavia, became a naturalized American citizen and a famous U.S. electrical inventor. Charles Steinmetz came here from Germany, handicapped by poverty and a physical deformity which made

him a lifelong cripple. As electrical engineer for General
Electric Company, he patented more than 100 inventions.

The famous John James Audubon was an immigrant
from Haiti. After several business failures, being jailed for debt
and taking bankruptcy, he published his unequaled collection
of paintings of American birds in their natural surroundings.

One of the many immigrants from Ireland was Father
Edward Flanagan, who came here as a young Catholic priest
and settled in Omaha, Nebraska. When he started his famous
Boys Town there, he borrowed the money for the first month's
rent on a house, and he begged door to door for the furniture to
put in it. Father Flanagan's Boys Home lived from hand to
mouth in material things, while he concentrated on giving
homeless boys what they needed most of all: spiritual values,
religion and human affection. Father Flanagan's Boys Town
grew and expanded, weathering one financial crisis after
another. By any standard, he was a tremendous success and one
of the great Americans of our century.

So, welcome to America, the land of freedom and
opportunity.

Unfortunately, when you read the daily press, you get a
rather different picture of our nation. You read of crime in the

streets and delinquency on the college campuses. You read of young men burning their draft cards and clergymen inciting people to do illegal acts. You read of the breakdown of moral values and of the tragic results of dope and drink. These problems are real, and they need correcting. We do have an increasing number of native parasites in our midst, unwashed, ungrateful for the privilege of living in America, and unwilling to defend it against its enemies.

These are a small but troublesome percentage of our people. Don't confuse them with the great majority of Americans who are good, law-abiding, and generous. One of the reasons why we are so glad to welcome you as new citizens is because you know and appreciate that America is a great county—and we can use your help in protecting our country against those who are trying to burn it down.

America is well worth defending. It is worth defending against the Communists and the Socialists who want to tie us down with the chains of past failures. America is worth defending against the criminals in our cities who have made our streets unsafe. America is worth defending against the tyrants in the Kremlin who have vowed to bury us and are building giant nuclear weapons capable of doing just that.

So, thank you, dear friends, for choosing America as your adopted land. We welcome you to our land of freedom and opportunity. We invite you to put your shoulder to the wheel to make sure America stays a land of freedom and opportunity—so that you can share this privilege with your children and with the other new citizens who will come after you.

Chapter 2
Copyrights and Censorship
June 1973

A few days ago, the Soviet Union formally adhered to the Universal Copyright Convention, and three cheers went up from the customary crowd which is always looking under the bed for new evidence of good will on the part of the Soviet rulers.

Everyone knows that, for decades, the Soviets have refused to respect international copyrights. They have systematically pirated books by Western authors and refused to pay any royalties.

For example, Sherlock Holmes is a top favorite with the reading Russian public. Several years ago, a Harvard Law School professor went to Moscow on behalf of the Conan Doyle estate to bring a court case to recover some of the royalties. He was able to produce the Soviet Government's own records which proved that tens of thousands of Sherlock Holmes books exist in Russian libraries. But it was a wasted trip; he got nowhere.

Soviet censorship is so thorough that the list of subjects which Russian writers are forbidden to mention runs to 300 pages. Included in the taboos is any mention of censorship itself. Some 70,000 censors are employed to enforce this censorship.

The new Soviet decision to join the Universal Copyright Convention does not indicate any change of heart. It proves only that the Soviets never sign an agreement unless there is some loophole which gives them a big advantage over other signers.

The Kremlin thought-control bosses just can't tolerate the literary success of Alexander Solzhenitsyn. Inside Russia, they can cope with his deviation from the Party line. They have banned his books, censored his mail, spied on this house, tapped his telephone, planted bugs in his apartment ceiling, carried on a persistent campaign of personal slander, and shadowed and beaten his friends.

The Soviets have not figured out a way to use our laws to help them ban the publication in the West of the writings of Solzhenitsyn and other Russian critics of Communism. By signing the Copyright Convention, the Soviets have acquired the right to go into American courts and enjoin Western publishers from printing the works of Russian authors without the consent of the copyright author—which is, of course, the Soviet Government.

The Soviets haven't changed their tune. They've just figured out a way to use our law enforcement facilities to enforce total control on Russian writers.

Chapter 3
How American Inventors
Changed the Way We Live
April 1988

By the American Revolution, our forefathers achieved independence for our tiny nation, plus political and religious liberty for each individual. However, economic conditions had changed very little in thousands of years. Then, suddenly, in the short space of 200 years, America experienced a tremendous explosion of human energy, an expansion of wealth, a rise in living standards that exceeded all the economic changes in the thousands of years that preceded our Constitution. Why did this happen?

Other countries have had men and women of great talent, such as Leonardo da Vinci. Natural resources have always been available on every continent. Crude oil oozed from the ground in biblical days, and Europe was full of untouched natural riches when Julius Caesar marched north from Rome.

What made America different was the magic ingredient of economic freedom guaranteed by the United States Constitution. The Founding Fathers, who wrote that great and original document 200 years ago, knew that economic freedom is just as important as our other God-given individual liberties.

Only if you are secure in the ownership of your personal property, and the right to choose your occupation, to quit your job and switch to another, can you attend the church of your choice, speak your mind and vote for your candidates, without fear of having your livelihood confiscated.

James Madison and Alexander Hamilton believed that the right of private property ranks with our most important personal liberties. The right of private property means you can retain the fruits of your labor for yourselves, your families and your children.

The Founding Fathers also understood how securing to individual inventors the right to own and market their original ideas is just as much a part of economic freedom as any other personal labor. The senior delegate at the Constitutional Convention, Benjamin Franklin, had invented such useful items as bifocals and a rocking chair, and had discovered electricity by his famous experiment of flying a kite in a storm.

Before the United States Constitution, there were no laws that gave an inventor the right to own his invention. English kings, depending on royal whim, would sometimes grant a monopoly over a product or process. Some American colonies and states had granted a few patents, but each inventor had to obtain a special act of the legislature. Then, on September 5, 1787, the Constitutional Convention adopted this provision: "The Congress shall have power ... to promote the progress of science and useful arts, by securing for limited times to authors and inventors the exclusive right to their respective writings and discoveries."

For the first time in history, a government recognized the right of inventors to profit from their inventions, instead of making them dependent on the political favor of a king or legislature. This uniquely American rule is completely democratic; it offers the same opportunity, the same protection, and the same hope of reward to every individual.

The unanimous adoption of this provision about inventors occurred a few days after the Convention delegates had recessed to watch experiments of the newly invented steamboat on the Delaware River.

Almost immediately after our new government was organized in 1789, inventors started making applications for patents. On April 10, 1790, President George Washington signed the Patent Act which established the distinctively American rule that inventions should be encouraged by guaranteeing to every inventor the exclusive right to his invention for a fixed term of years, after which the public is free to use it. The law rejected the idea that patents should be licensed or taxed, as many other countries do. The law requires only that the inventor file a full description of his invention and how it works, with specifications and drawings.

This right of private property attracted talent and capital to invest in inventions that have given us a fantastic increase in our living standards and made America the industrial and technological leader of the world.

No other nation has had such a remarkable series of inventions. But then, no other nation has enjoyed the stimulus to inventions provided by a free economy.

It is appropriate that Thomas Jefferson was the first Administrator of the American Patent System. He personally examined all the applications that came before the Board.

"Nobody wishes more than I do," Jefferson said, "that ingenuity should receive liberal encouragement."

Jefferson was a mathematician, astronomer, architect, inventor, and the most versatile intellect of his time. His inventions included an improvement in the plough which was helpful to farming, a revolving chair which his enemies accused him of designing "so as to look all ways at once," and a folding chair that doubled as a walking stick.

Before Jefferson died, he was able to say: "The issue of patents for new discoveries has given a spring to inventions beyond my conception." One generation later, the French commentator Alexis de Tocqueville called America "a land of wonders in which everything is in constant motion and every change seems an improvement."

Let's consider the major inventions that rolled out of the creative minds of Americans in the new climate of freedom created by our Constitution.

AGRICULTURE

Hunger was a normal condition of life for most people who have lived on Planet Earth, and millions have starved to death in every century. Only the United States has never had a famine, and even our poorest people can eat abundantly.

Yet, we started out just as poor as any other nation. At the time our Constitution was written, American farmers felled the trees, tilled the soil, and ground the grain with the same crude tools that men had used for thousands of years. Then, after our Constitution was adopted, things began to change almost immediately!

In 1793, Eli Whitney received a patent for his cotton gin, a device to mechanically separate the seeds from cotton fiber. That one machine replaced the hand labor of four dozen men, revolutionized cotton harvesting, and made cotton commercially profitable. This created prosperity for the southern states that grew cotton, and prosperity for the northern states that manufactured the cloth.

Cyrus McCormick of Virginia took farming one big step further when he received a patent for his reaper in 1829. From the dawn of history, grain had been cut with a hand sickle. McCormick's reaper enabled farmers to harvest wheat by machine instead of by hand, so a farmer could harvest seven acres of grain in a day instead of only the half acre he could cut by hand. At first, McCormick's reaper was drawn by horses;

then it was powered by a steam engine. This invention changed the whole world because grain is our most common food.

McCormick's reaper came at just the time when the Mississippi River Valley began to be settled. It assured Americans of an endless supply of cereals from the great plains of the Midwest. Much of our country's wealth began to come from the "amber waves of grain" made possible by McCormick's reaper. Today our grain is harvested by very sophisticated farm vehicles.

In 1846, when horses were still the main source of power on the farm, a midwestern blacksmith named John Deere invented a plow with a steel wearing surface. This new plow solved the problem of soil sticking to iron plows, thereby helping the farmer to "plow ahead!"

Twenty years later, James Oliver of Iowa developed an iron plow with a face that was hardened by being chilled in the mold when it was cast. When Oliver died in 1908 he was the richest man in Iowa, and his invention had tremendously enriched all American farmers.

Joseph Glidden of Illinois invented what he called an "improvement in wire fences" in 1873. Today we call his invention barbed wire. Glidden's ingenuity provided a cheap and efficient way to fence our vast western farm lands.

Throughout the late 1880s, American inventors continued their improvements in farm equipment. They invented devices for breaking up lumps in the soil and for planting seeds. They invented threshing machines and combines for processing an entire crop. In 1886, a New Jersey farm woman, Anna Baldwin, invented the first suction milking machine. In the 20th century, gasoline tractors took the place of steam driven machines, and the mechanization of agriculture began driving full speed ahead.

One of America's most industrious inventors around the turn of the century was George Washington Carver. He invented 300 uses for the peanut, including oil used for medicines and dyes, and by-products for breakfast foods and face creams. And can you imagine a world without peanut butter? Carver made the peanut one of our chief crops and greatly helped the economy of the south.

When Soviet boss Nikita Khrushchev came to America in 1959, he most of all wanted to see the marvelously productive American farms. When he was taken to a farm in Iowa, Khrushchev couldn't resist saying, "Where are all the workers?" He simply could not believe that one farmer could cultivate and harvest so much land all by himself.

Why is American agriculture the envy of the world, providing Americans with an endless variety of fresh foods in winter as well as summer, our grain bins overflowing, and enough left over to feed millions in other lands? It's because of the magic ingredient of economic freedom that has encouraged inventors to create, and investors to manufacture, such marvelous modern farm machines.

COMMUNICATION

The need to communicate between the large distances of our new nation was a tremendous challenge. At the time our country was founded, the fastest way to send a message between one town and another was typified by the horseback ride of Paul Revere. Soon, creative minds began to prove that America is, indeed, "a land of wonders."

A pioneer in communications was Samuel Morse, who received a patent in 1840 for what he called "Telegraph Signs," a method of sending messages over wire. His invention made possible instantaneous communications between distant points. On May 24, 1844, Morse himself sent the first telegram from

Washington, D.C., to Baltimore. It was the famous message, "What hath God wrought."

Foreign inventors also recognized the value of the U.S. patent system. In 1887, the Italian, Marconi, received an American patent for his wireless telegraph. Soon we were able to send wireless messages across the Atlantic Ocean.

The legendary Alexander Graham Bell received a patent for the telephone in 1876. No other invention was ever taken up so quickly and by so many people. From the first clumsy telephone over which it was often difficult to hear, and which was manually handled by a crude switchboard, the telephone has developed into one of the most sophisticated and efficient of all our modem conveniences. Now we can direct-dial almost anywhere in the world, and the speed and the clarity of sound are almost magical.

America's greatest inventor, Thomas A. Edison of Menlo Park, New Jersey, gave us the phonograph. To hear the human voice coming from a record seemed like a miracle to Edison's generation. The puzzled look on the dog's face when he heard "His Master's Voice" coming out of a record player became a famous advertisement, and the old hand-cranked victorola became a household treasure. Another of Edison's important inventions was motion pictures. We even have a picture of Edison using the camera himself.

It was Edison who created the idea of a laboratory in which a team of people works fulltime on inventions. Despite only three months of formal schooling, Edison was our greatest inventive genius and patented more than a thousand inventions.

In 1868, Charles Sholes, editor of a Milwaukee newspaper, received a patent for the first typewriter, thereby creating a tremendous new source of jobs for women. Typewriters are better and faster today, but their keyboards are just the same.

More Americans began to read the printed word after Ottmar Mergentheler of Baltimore received a patent in 1884 for a typesetting machine that could set a whole line of type in one solid block. His line-o-type printing press made possible the cheap and rapid printing of newspapers, magazines and books.

In the 1880s, George Eastman invented the first Kodak camera. Prior to Eastman, all cameras required a tripod. Eastman's invention enabled amateurs to take snapshots, and millions of Americans have been preserving precious memories on film ever since. "You press the button-we do the rest." became a household slogan.

The Polaroid camera invented by Edwin Land came along in 1947. Then we could take instant 60-second pictures.

In 1893. Frederic Ives of Philadelphia received a patent for a "photogravure" printing plate. Pictures in newspapers became, first a curiosity, then customary. You remember the line from Irving Berlin's song, "Easter Parade": "You'll find that you're in the rotogravure." In Berlin's day, it was "special" to see pictures of women in their Easter Bonnets in the Sunday newspaper.

One of the most remarkable inventors of our time was Chester Carlson who invented the xerox copy. That means copying documents by a dry, electrical process onto plain paper instead of by the traditional wet, photographic process. While working a full-time, $35-a-week job during the Great Depression, he spent his evenings in the public library and, to his wife's dismay, conducted experiments in their kitchen. On October 22. 1938. Carlson invented xeroxing when he successfully transferred an image of that day's date onto a piece of paper.

It took Carlson 20 years to persuade anyone to invest the money to develop his new idea into a useful product. Then, the first xerox copier became one of the most successful single products ever made. Today, a copier is as indispensable to every office as a typewriter and a telephone.

The year 1907 marked a great turning point in radio communication when Lee DeForest, one of the "fathers of radio," patented a vacuum tube called an audion. This tube, which amplified weak sounds, was an invention as great as radio itself because it made possible long-distance radio and television communication. The first musical radio broadcast in history featured Caruso singing from backstage of the Metropolitan Opera House in 1910.

The entertainment field went through many changes in the early 20th century. In the mid-1920s, Bell Labs developed a new system that successfully coordinated sound on records with a movie projector. In the movie called "The Jazz Singer," the famous entertainer Al Jolson spoke a few lines and sang. That ended the era of silent films and started what were called "talkies." Vladimir Zworykin demonstrated the first practical television set in 1929. He invented the television tube suitable for broadcasting and the picture tube in a television receiver.

In 1947, the transistor, one of the most important inventions of the 20th century, was developed by a group at Bell Labs headed by William Shockley. A transistor is a miniature device to control the flow of electric current. It replaced the bulky and unreliable vacuum tube.

Before the 1960s, radios were big and heavy, and, when we turned them on, there was a delay before we heard any sound. When radios were made with transistors, they became smaller, lighter weight and portable, with instantaneous sound.

Transistors were an essential part of the gigantic expansion of our telephone communications system. In 1940, someone estimated that, if telephone usage continued to expand, within 30 years every woman in the United States would be a telephone operator! Fortunately, automatic equipment replaced telephone operators, and the transistor did the work that those millions of women would have done.

The effect of the transistor on computers was even more spectacular. The analog computer was invented by Vannevar Bush in 1930, but for 20 years computers were made with those big, unreliable vacuum tubes. Then came the transistor.

In the 1960s, our engineers learned how to put several transistors on a chip of silicon the size of a fingernail. In the capitalist climate of Silicon Valley, California, new companies competed with each other to develop improvements. Now, a million transistors can be put on a one-inch-square silicon chip. As the size goes down, the speed and reliability increase, and the cost goes down. More than 25 million computers are in use in America today, in offices, schools, and homes.

TRANSPORTATION.

Just as great American inventors developed new ways of talking over long distances, so they also invented new ways of transporting people and freight from here to there. When our Constitution was written, the need to travel vast distances was one of our greatest challenges.

In 1789, John Fitch built the first steamboat. He used steam power to propel a rowboat and established regular steamboat passenger service on the Delaware River.

Another American, Robert Fulton, invented the first practical steamship in 1807. It was a great hit in America, but Europeans didn't understand this new-fangled device. For example, Fulton got an appointment with Napoleon to try to sell him on the idea of a steamboat to use in his battles with Britain. Fulton spread out his designs and models and explained how, on a day with no wind, Napoleon could defeat the English navy of sailboats, and then move the French army across the English Channel on steamboats. But Napoleon didn't see the value; he literally missed the boat.

In 1849 a young Congressman from Illinois, Abraham Lincoln, as a result of his river experience, invented "a device for buoying vessels over shoals and sandbars." Lincoln whittled the model for his application with his own hands. In a lecture in Springfield, Illinois, Lincoln spoke the much-quoted line: "The patent system added the fuel of interest to the fire of genius."

For years, train travel was the principal method of transportation for most Americans. After George Pullman invented the Pullman traveling train car in 1858, passengers could ride in comfort and style. The Pullman car remained a vital part of our transportation system until the 1950s, and it's sad that the younger generation in America will never know how exciting it was to travel in a Pullman.

Americans of all ages can still enjoy the bicycle, thanks to Pierre Lallement, a French carriage maker, who took out a U.S. patent on a pedal bicycle in 1866.

One of the most important transportation advances of all time came in 1869 when George Westinghouse of Schenectady invented the air brake for railroad cars. This invention enabled the engineer of the train to control the brakes himself, using compressed air, rather than relying on brakemen. The air brake made it possible for trains to be longer and faster, thus enabling railroads to handle the passenger and freight traffic of our expanding nation.

The air brake was soon followed by a patent for railroad "car couplings" invented by Eli Janney of Virginia. Before Janney, railroad cars had to be coupled by a brakeman going between the cars and manually linking them while the engineer gently pushed the cars together—a very dangerous process that killed or injured hundreds of men. The automatic car coupler saved lives, limbs and time. Trains improved in comfort and speed as they carried our nation into the 20th century.

The automobile age was born in 1899 when Ransom Olds invented the first affordable automobile. Olds conceived the idea of an inexpensive auto for everybody and sold what he called a "runabout" for $650. It cost $25 more to get a top on your car.

In 1898, Henry Ford of Detroit received his first of 161 patents. It was for carburetors. He introduced his Model T Ford in 1906; it was cheap, rugged, and dominated the American market for 20 years. Henry Ford is especially known for developing the modern methods of mass production with interchangeable parts, the assembly lines, and finally the conveyor assembly.

At first, each driver had to hand crank his car to start it. Driving certainly was made easier when Charles Ketiering invented the electric self-starter for automobiles in 1911.

Rubber tires immediately became essential for automobiles, using a process invented by Charles Goodyear. Today's tires not only have to work for the family, but for sports and industry as well. Rubber is used to make the snug wrap on our lettuce and is essential to pipelines carrying oil across vast distances. When Voyager made its nonstop flight around the world, it too used rubber tires. The new rubber became indispensable not only for automobiles, but for consumer products such as footwear, waterproof garments, fire hoses, and rubber bands.

Americans were on the move—in trains, automobiles, and streetcars.

But Americans would not be tied to the ground. When two brothers who ran a bicycle shop in Dayton, Ohio, took to the sky at Kitty Hawk, North Carolina, the whole world of transportation took off with them. Solemnly told by the Smithsonian Institution that air flight was impossible, Orville and Wilbur Wright proceeded with their experiments and were among the first to apply scientific methodology to inventions. In 1906, the Wright Brothers received a patent for what they called "new and useful improvements in Flying Machines." Their great invention changed our lives.

Charles Lindbergh's New York-to-Paris flight in 1927 thrilled the world and dramatized America's world leadership in aviation. Even the helicopter was invented in America by Igor Sikorsky in 1939.

Since then, we have made gigantic leaps into the era of modern jets, to the Voyager that flew nonstop around the earth, to the shuttle that takes astronauts to outer space. From the covered wagons that carried Americans to the Western frontier, to the space ships that carried our astronauts to the moon, is a long way to go in 200 years—farther and faster than the whole

world had gone in the previous 10,000 years. But then, those
other nations didn't have the magic ingredient of economic
freedom which has stimulated so much creative talent in
America.

HOME

Of all the changes that have come about in America, the
"land of wonders," none is so dramatic as the change in the
comforts of home. For thousands of years of recorded history,
most people lived in floorless, windowless, dark, little hovels
or caves.

When our Constitution was written, American women
cooked over an open fire, just as women had cooked since
history began. Housewives carried water from a spring or well,
made their own soap, and made the candles that provided
meager light for the long hours of darkness. American wives
and mothers in those days not only made all the family's
clothes, but they spun the thread and wove the coarse cloth
with a spindle and loom like those used by the ancient
Egyptians.

After Eli Whitney's cotton gin made cotton cloth cheap
and abundant, women no longer had to spend every evening

spinning and weaving cloth for their families. Women got an evening off from their duties every now and then.

In 1842, Elias Howe of Cambridge, Massachusetts, received a patent for his sewing machine, which he called a "new and useful machine for sewing seams in cloth or other articles," and Isaac Singer patented improvements. It is impossible to overestimate how the sewing machine lightened the work load of the average woman.

In the 1890s, James Northrup invented the first completely automatic loom, and Whitcomb Judson invented what he called the "slide fastener" and we call the zipper.

In 1849, Walter Hunt invented the modern safety pin. I can't imagine what it must have been like diapering babies in the hundreds of years before the safety pin was invented.

Mark Twain was an inventor, too. He received a patent for a Self-Pasting Scrapbook in 1873. This was a series of blank pages coated with gum. He sold 25,000 copies, which led one newspaper to say, that was pretty good for "a book that did not contain a single word that critics could praise or condemn."

Traditional wood-burning stoves and fireplaces began to be replaced when Jordan Mott invented the first practical coal stove in 1833. Called a baseburner, this stove had ventilation so it could burn coal efficiently. Cooking has been getting easier ever since.

A distinctive American contribution to heating technology was the radiator, invented by William Baldwin. His cast iron radiators brought central heating into the homes of most Americans by the start of the 20th century.

The best friend women ever had was Thomas A. Edison, who received a patent in 1880 for what he called "an electric lamp for giving light by incandescence." No other invention changed the lives of so many people as the electric light bulb. At the beginning, light bulbs were sold door-to-door from horse drawn wagons. By the 1930s, new houses came already wired with electricity! Today, every American home has electric light, and modern kitchens are filled with a dazzling variety of electric appliances, especially refrigerators, stoves, and ovens.

When Alva Fisher invented the electric washing machine in 1910, he rescued women from the backbreaking burden of doing the family laundry by hand. Washing machines steadily improved, and we really appreciate those improvements.

In 1886, Schulyer Wheeler invented the electric fan, a principal method of home cooling until Willis Haviland Carrier, the father of air conditioning, designed the first scientific system to clean, circulate and control the temperature and humidity of air.

When it comes to keeping cool, Americans can even take credit for the ice cream cone. It was invented at the St. Louis World's Fair in 1904.

A process called frosted foods was invented by Clarence Birdseye. It was an instant success and, today, frozen foods are part of our way of life. Fifty years ago, the ice man used to come every day and deliver blocks of ice to home "ice boxes" so we could keep our foods from spoiling. Today's refrigerators enable us to preserve food for weeks at a time. Whereas the daily lot of women in other lands is to stand in line, for food and other essentials which are always in scarce supply, refrigeration enables American women to shop at supermarkets once a week, and enjoy perishable produce every month of the year.

INDUSTRY AND ENERGY

Meanwhile, other inventions were creating new American industries and the energy to provide power to those industries.

J. J. Ritty invented the cash register in 1879, just in time to ring up the profits on one of the greatest decades in the history of inventions. The 1880s gave us the light bulb, the street car, the automobile, the pneumatic tire, electrical welding, the steam turbine, the electric furnace, and Nikola Tesla's alternating-current motor which was the start of the electric motor. It was an incredible decade!

In 1869, John Wesley Hyatt, a printer in Albany, New York, tried to win a $10,000 prize offered for a substitute for ivory to make billiard balls. What he discovered was Celluloid, the first synthetic plastics material to be widely used commercially. It soon was used in making collars, dentures, combs, and photographic film.

Chemist Leo Baekeland, a chemist of Yonkers, New York, invented the first synthetic resin called Bakelite in 1909. Bakelite became widely used to make telephones and handles for pots and irons, and it laid the foundation of the giant modem plastics industry.

In 1889, Charles Hall of Oberlin, Ohio, received a patent for the first inexpensive method to produce aluminum. This gave birth to our great aluminum industry.

Americans devised new and ingenious ways to drive across our nation's rivers. John Roebling invented the suspension bridge used in 1869 to build the Brooklyn Bridge, which became known as the eighth wonder of the world. Captain James Eads designed the world's first steel arch bridge and built Eads bridge across the Mississippi River at St. Louis in 1874. This railroad bridge opened up our great transcontinental railway system.

In 1902, George Fuller invented the first steel skyscraper, the 21-story Flatiron Building in New York City. His original design was based on a steel cage. Fuller went ahead despite dire predictions that wind and weight would make his skyscraper collapse. Today more than half our large office and apartment buildings are copied from Fuller's steel cage design. Very tall buildings were built before America was founded, but the pyramids depended on slave labor, and the great European cathedrals depended on religious dedication, and each building took at least a generation to build. It took an American inventor to make tall buildings economical and practical for commercial life, and they became the heart of our modem cities.

Nylon, invented by the DuPont Company in 1939, was the first synthetic fabric that was superior to natural fabrics. This great chemical discovery started a whole new industry. It was a great day for women when we started to wear long-lasting nylons instead of fragile silk stockings.

The story of how the slide rule was replaced by the pocket calculator is a great lesson in how our American competitive system brings consumer prices down. When the calculator first came on the market about 1970, it sold for hundreds of dollars. Now, a powerful calculator sells for no more than a slide rule used to cost, but the calculator does so much more work, so much faster, that it saves years of time in the life of any engineer.

The peaceful use of nuclear energy is 20th century America's contribution to energy production. In 1942 Enrico Fermi and several fellow scientists conducted the first atomic energy experiment on the football field of the University of Chicago. Nuclear energy is the cheapest, cleanest and safest source of electric power today. The city of Chicago, for example, is fortunate to get 60 percent of its electricity from nuclear energy plants. The United States has 90 nuclear plants operating today. Without them we would have to import billions of barrels of expensive foreign oil to make our electricity.

Now, industry is developing new products using lasers. The compact disks can play all our favorite music with perfect fidelity. Who knows what exciting new products will be produced by American industries in the future?

MILITARY

Our economic prosperity depends absolutely on our military power to protect it. Our high standard of living and unparalleled prosperity rest inescapably on our ability to keep aggressors from conquering our people, stealing our products, and invading our homeland.

American military strength is due not only to the courage and stamina of our fighting men as they demonstrated on D-Day and time and time again. What has made America superior in military strength is the quality and quantity of the weapons and equipment with which they were provided by a prosperous and supportive nation. Creative men have invented and developed new technologies, new processes, and better weapons. Our great industrial strength has produced new weapons, such as the Trident nuclear submarine, in the quality and quantity needed to meet every military challenge.

The same man who created and patented the first important invention after our Constitution was adopted, Eli Whitney of cotton gin fame, was, through the influence of Thomas Jefferson, given a government contract to build 10,000 muskets for the War Department. Before that time, guns had always been built by hand, each part laboriously filed and fitted together by skilled gunsmiths. Each worker made everything from the stock to the trigger. Whitney had an original idea. He thought that, if he could make standard parts, then parts of a gun would be interchangeable, and a gun could be repaired right on the battlefield. This sounds obvious today, but it was a new idea when Whitney pioneered it. Eli Whitney built his 10,000 muskets in time for the United States to defeat the British redcoats in the War of 1812. Whitney had laid the foundation for quantity production of complex military and civilian products.

In 1829 Samuel Colt of Hartford, Connecticut, invented the first revolver, a six-shooter pistol. He was only 16 years old when he whittled his model out of a wooden block. His six-shooter played a big role in our winning of the West and in our War with Mexico.

John Ericsson, a brilliant engineer who came here from Sweden, designed the ironclad Monitor in time to save the Union Navy in a great battle with the Confederate Merrimack in 1862. The Monitor used more than 40 Ericsson inventions. Abraham Lincoln was a great booster of inventions, and the Monitor might not have been built without President Lincoln's insistence.

In 1861, Richard Gatling of Indianapolis invented the first practical machine gun. Ten barrels were rotated around a central axis by turning a crank, so that a strong gunner could fire as many as 1,200 shots a minute.

Other Civil War inventions included military balloons, land mines, and torpedoes. Incidentally, Clara Barton was employed by the U.S. Patent Office before she had the ingenious idea during the Civil War of founding the American Red Cross. She was one of the first women employed by the Federal Government.

In 1881, John Holland, a schoolteacher who had immigrated here from Ireland, invented the first modern submarine. The Navy advertised for designs, and his was accepted. His boat, called the Plunger, was a big success.

The years of World War I showed the world the American genius of workshop and factory. We made great technological advances in guns, artillery, mortars, tanks, and sea mines. America developed the Liberty engine for fighter planes and made big advances in radio communications. We made the best gas masks in World War I. Our chemists discovered methods to prevent meat spoilage and to dehydrate foods, and one of the popular products to come out of World War I was instant coffee!

Americans insured victory for the allies by sending munitions and supplies in time and in ample supply.

The inventions during World War II were just as remarkable. Probably the most significant, except for the atomic bomb, was the proximity fuse which explodes without actual contact as it nears its target. Americans have played a major role in developing and refining radar, one of the winning weapons of World War II.

HEALTH

The creative genius unleased by the Constitution has been responsible for tremendous inventions to cure disease, save lives, and lengthen the healthy life span of Americans to 75 years.

Prior to the 20th century, a soldier with a battle wound had a small chance of surviving and had no anesthetics for his pain. By World War II, our servicemen had sulfa drugs, blood transfusions, and anesthetics available for immediate use.

When we tried to build the Panama Canal at the start of this century, yellow fever killed the workers faster than they could build the Canal. The Americans discovered that the mosquito carried yellow fever, figured out how to control it, and then built the great Canal.

In 1900, Hoffman received a patent on aspirin, still the most widely-used pain-killer. There was no real treatment for arthritis until the doctors at the Mayo Clinic in Minnesota discovered a drug that would help. The polio virus killed or crippled thousands of Americans, including President Franklin D. Roosevelt. Polio is no longer a threat, thanks to the vaccines invented by Dr. Jonas Salk and Dr. Albert Sabin.

Prior to World War II, there was no generally effective drug to fight infection. Now, the great killer diseases, such as tuberculosis, typhoid fever, scarlet fever, influenza, pneumonia, and blood poisoning are routinely cured by drugs. Lives of children and adults all over the world have been saved by the wonder drugs: first the sulfa drugs, then the antibiotics including penicillin.

Nine out of ten prescriptions today call for drugs that did not exist 40 years ago. Our patent system protects both the inventor and the costly investments in laboratory research that make the wonder drugs available at reasonable cost.

CONCLUSION

Our Constitution gave America a wonderful system for protecting the labor and work-product of inventors, fostering industrial and technical progress, and ultimately letting the world benefit from individual genius. We've seen the spectacular results. America has only 5 percent of the world's population, but our "land of wonders" has created more new wealth than all other nations in the world combined.

The drawings of Leonardo da Vinci in the 15th century prove that some great inventors are not American. Leonardo's inventions included an automobile, an airplane, a parachute, a movable bridge, and a multi-barrel gun. But his inventions existed only on paper. Only in America could such ideas actually be built, where men are free to invent and to invest in the certainty that they will own the product on which they pour out their talent, skill, and financial resources.

President Dwight D. Eisenhower said: "This system has for years encouraged the imaginative to dream and to experiment—in garages and sheds, in great universities and corporate laboratories. Innovations and discoveries ... have created new industries ... giving more and more Americans better jobs and adding greatly to the prosperity and well-being of all."

The greatest of all American inventions is the Constitution itself. It was an original design that came from the creative minds of a very remarkable group of men who had fought for liberty, understood how precious it is, and built an instrument that has endured for 200 years.

In freedom, the future is more exciting than our best minds can predict. We have every reason to believe that America's next 200 years will be as great or greater than our past—so long as we keep the economic liberty designed by our great United States Constitution.

Chapter 4
Protect Our Constitutional Patent Rights
July 1996

One of our most important constitutional rights is the right of inventors to have, for limited times, "the exclusive right to their ... discoveries." This uniquely American provision in Article I, Section 8 of the U.S. Constitution marked a profound turning point in world history.

Most of the world's inventions are American, and they have proved an essential factor in American economic growth and prosperity. Our marvelous inventions are fundamental to our enviable standard of living and to building America into an industrial super power.

Our basic constitutional patent right is now under attack from the lobbyists for Japanese and multinational corporations. It would be wiped out by a bill that has already passed the House Judiciary Committee and is rushing toward a vote in the House.

H.R. 3460 would order the publication of all inventors' patent applications 18 months after the application is filed, whether or not the inventor has yet been (or will ever be) granted a patent. This would be a dramatic change from our traditional treatment of patents and would be a grievous injustice to the individual inventor.

Inventors' patent applications have always been held in total secrecy by the U.S. Patent Office until the patent is issued, thus safeguarding the exclusive right of the inventor. It is kept secret forever if he is not granted a patent, so the inventor can continue his work without someone stealing his ideas while they are developing.

Publication of the application before the patent is issued would be a tremendous giveaway to foreign and big corporation competitors. They could use their enormous resources against the individual inventor to challenge and invalidate a patent application before it is granted, or to steal the idea and beat the individual in getting a patent and going into production with it.

H.R. 3460 would make the U.S. Patent Office a private corporation, inevitably putting all future policies and regulations about patents under control of the giant corporations. This would freeze the individual inventor and all small entities out of the invention process, wiping out their constitutional patent rights.

H.R. 3460 would allow outside parties, including foreign entities, to challenge all existing U.S. patents in a reexamination process conducted by the U.S. Patent Office rather than in the courts. Previously, once a patent was issued, the invention itself and its claims could not be challenged in the Patent Office without a showing of prior descriptive material about the invention of which the Patent Office was unaware when it issued the patent.

This dramatic change from past procedure would make it easier and far cheaper for outside parties to invalidate a patent. This change would also impede enforcement of the inventor's patent rights because the courts usually suspend patent enforcement litigation while a reexamination is in progress.

H.R. 3460 would thus amount to a major power shift from the courts to the Patent Office. Foreign and multinational corporations might prefer this, but the individual inventor would lose his traditional protections of due process, rules of evidence, and jury trial.

H.R. 3460 is sponsored by Rep. Carlos Moorhead (R-CA) and Rep. Patricia Schroeder (D-CO), the ranking members of the two parties on the Intellectual Property Subcommittee. Both are retiring from Congress this year and will then be available to lobby for the big corporations and foreign interests that will benefit from this bill.

Passage of the Moorhead-Schroeder legislative swan song would bugle taps for the American dream. It would undermine our job base, prevent new companies from forming, and limit our future growth.

Many great American companies, including General Electric, AT&T, Kodak, International Harvester, B.F. Goodrich, Goodyear Tire, Polaroid, John Deere, Westinghouse, and Xerox exist today because the patents issued to their founders gave them exclusive ownership for enough time to start their businesses.

Another serious infringement of inventors' patent rights was concealed in the fine print of the GATT Agreement, passed by Congress in the infamous lame duck session of November 1994. This changed the term of exclusivity granted by a patent from 17 years from date of issuance of the patent to 20 years from the date of application.

This curtails inventors' patent rights in cases where the processing of the patent application suffers delay. The Patent Office may be dilatory in processing the application, big corporations may falsely assert ownership of the patent, or the process may be slowed by the harassing litigation made possible by H.R. 3460.

Fortunately, some Congressmen are alert to the interferences with patent rights under both GATT and the Moorhead-Schroeder bill. Rep. Dana Rohrabacher (R-CA), with 55 cosponsors, is pressing for a vote on H.R. 359. It would correct the mistake in the GATT Agreement by making the term of patents the longer of either 17 years from the date the patent is issued OR 20 years from the date the application was filed.

In introducing the companion bill in the Senate, S. 284, Bob Dole said, "Our inventors and creative Americans all over the country deserve the maximum protection of their intellectual property. We should not jeopardize their investment in ideas. The new [GATT] rule threatens that investment. [We must] restore the most important aspect of an inventor's livelihood: the period of time he owns his invention."

Chapter 5
Who's Interfering with Our
Constitutional Patent Rights?
April 1997

Y ou would think that federal officeholders wouldn't touch with a ten-foot pole anything that might be connected in any way with the use of Asian money to influence government policies. So much suspect Asian money has had to be returned to its donors during the last six months.

Yet, the House is getting ready to vote on a bill that would make the granting of U.S. patents a prime target for Asian bribes. The sponsors of H.R. 400 call it the Patent Improvement Act, but it should be called the Patent Giveaway bill, the Steal American Technology bill, or the Ron Brown Sellout Legacy.

H.R. 400 would transform the U.S. Patent Office into a private corporation that could accept bribes for the issuing of patents. Of course, the bill doesn't use the nasty word bribes; it just says that the newly privatized Patent Office "may accept monetary gifts or donations of services, or of real, personal, or mixed property, in order to carry out the functions of the Office."

With all the important business that Congress has to deal with, and the hundreds of bills that are awaiting action, it is a puzzlement that this bill is rushing to a vote in April. Where is the pressure coming from? And why hasn't there been any news coverage of this "stealth" bill?

A lot of the big pressure is coming from the Japanese— and from a quiet deal they made with the late Secretary of Commerce Ron Brown. In September 1993, the Japan Patent Association issued a written statement saying that it finds the U.S. patent system and patent legislation "unsatisfactory." What impudence! Our American patent system certainly doesn't have to conform to what the Japanese think is "satisfactory." Furthermore, it is almost impossible for an American inventor to get patent protection in the Japanese patent system.

The Japanese statement specifically objected to the fact that U.S. patent applications are not made public until the patent is issued. This is a fundamental protection for the inventor so that wealthy corporations, foreign or domestic, cannot steal his invention before he has a chance to raise his own capital to produce it.

The Japanese and the multinational corporations don't like this protection for inventors. They want access to American inventions before the patents are issued so they can steal them.

Hence, their demand that applications be made public 18 months after full application is filed regardless of whether or not a patent is issued. They argue that this is the way other countries do it and the United States should conform.

But so what! Other countries have hardly any inventions. Nearly all the great inventions are American. Inventions don't happen in socialist or managed economies.

Our fantastic American inventions are the result, not only of our free enterprise system, but especially of the unique American constitutional right of inventors to have, for limited times, "the exclusive right to their ... discoveries." The inventor's private property right in the fruit of his own labor is the "engine" that has stimulated the wonderful inventions that have caused our tremendous economic growth and rise in our standard of living.

Communist China has made a major business of stealing our intellectual property outright and mass-producing it in government-controlled factories. The Japanese just want to make it legal for them to get our inventions by bribery and, indeed, bribery is the ordinary system of doing business in many nations.

On August 16, 1994, a U.S. Commerce Department news release announced that Ron Brown had signed "Letters of Agreement" in his office with Japanese Ambassador Takakazu Kuriyama promising the Japanese exactly what they demanded. The news release stated that the Brown agreement "requires the U.S. Patent and Trademark Office to publish pending patent applications 18 months after filing ... and expand reexamination proceedings to allow greater participation by third parties."

Ambassador Kuriyama was ecstatic. He immediately wrote Ron Brown that "we look forward to working with you on a regular basis ... in the field of intellectual property." The purpose of H.R. 400 is to write the Japanese demands and Ron Brown's agreement into U.S. law.

The entire text of H.R. 400 is a sellout to the Japanese demands. H.R. 400 loosens up the "reexamination" of U.S.

patents already issued and allows third parties (e.g., foreign or domestic corporations) to participate in the process after paying a "reexamination fee." The inventor would lose the due process rights he would enjoy in U.S. courts, a caving in to Japanese objections to American jury trials.

H.R. 400 specifies that the board of directors of the new private patent office shall include persons "with substantial background and achievement in corporate finance and management." You can bet that some of the big multinationals are behind that provision, which would ride roughshod over the rights of individual inventors.

Ron Brown was at the center of the Clinton Administration's strategy of selling out American interests to the Asians in return for political cash to assure Clinton's reelection. Any Republican who votes for H.R. 400 is going to be tarred with the same Asian money scandal that is fast closing in on the Clinton Administration.

Chapter 6
Hatch's Attack on Inventor's
Constitutional Rights
July 1997

Fast track for NAFTA expansion, Most Favored Nation status for China, and foreign aid are all issues that pit the internationalist ideologues and multinationals against grassroots Americans and small business. But the issue that marks this division most clearly is the Ominous Patent bill (oops, the Omnibus Patent bill), S. 507.

The United States has produced more than 90 percent of the world's inventions because our patent system is superior to every other country's. Other countries that want to steal or copy our technology, and the multinationals that want to curry favor with foreign markets, are demanding that we change our system.

Senator Orrin Hatch's sponsorship of this bill is one more instance of his puzzling lurch to the left, along with collaborating on Kennedy KidCare and expediting Clinton's liberal court nominees. Hatch has rushed a slightly amended S. 507 through his Judiciary Committee.

Senate Small Business Committee Chairman Kit Bond (R-MO) is circulating a Dear Colleague letter pointing out that, even as amended, S. 507 will "jeopardize the value, certainty and protection of the American patent, threatening the ability of independent inventors and small businesses to continue their incredible work." Here is why.

Hatch's bill would greatly expand the procedures for reexamination of all existing patents, making it much easier for foreign and domestic corporations to challenge a patent immediately and invalidate patents already issued. This would dramatically decrease the existing rights of all current U.S. patent holders.

Challenging and defending a patent are very expensive processes. Forcing the inventor to defend his patent in a second examination puts a very costly burden on inventors and small businesses and would be a significant advantage to deep-pocket corporations. As Senator Bond explains, this "will destroy the certainty of a patent that is critical for the small guy to attract investors."

Hatch's bill would undercut our whole patent system by creating a new defense for patent infringers called "prior use." This would exempt from the payment of royalties an infringer who asserts he was using the idea before it was patented, thereby diluting the U.S. patent holder's constitutional "exclusive right."

Small businesses that have spent time and money creating a new idea and bringing it to market would thus have the value of their patent dramatically reduced. The advantage would shift to the big firms that poach on the ideas of individuals, then use large legal resources to avoid the patent process and the payment of royalties.

Hatch's bill would change the patent office from a government agency to a corporation with an outside board of directors and employees excluded from civil service. Hatch's big-business bias is painfully obvious: the text of S. 507 actually states that the directors shall include "individuals" (in the plural) with "achievement" in "corporate finance and management."

In his amendment, Hatch agreed to allow one member of the board to be an independent inventor; but, as Senator Bond points out, no space is reserved for a small business representative. Hatch's gesture is tokenism, and it certainly does not protect inventors' rights.

The bill would even allow corporations to influence the patent office through "gifts" (a.k.a. bribes). Hatch bragged in his press release that he "accommodated the Administration" by "fend[ing] off the unjustified but politically appealing attacks on the corporation's gift provision."

Hatch's S. 507 as originally introduced would have eliminated our traditional rule that all patent applications remain secret unless and until a patent is actually issued. Although the amended S. 507 now includes a limited exception for U.S. inventors willing to forgo applying for a foreign patent, early publication was and is the primary goal of the extraordinary lobbying effort to change our patent system being made by the Japanese, the multinationals and the Clinton Administration.

Senator Bond accurately points out that the initial secrecy about an invention is "the cornerstone of our patent system" because it preserves the property right of the inventor until he gets his legal rights recognized in a patent. Publication of the details of an invention before a patent is issued would set it up to be stolen by infringers and copycats all over the world who are, as Bond says, just "waiting around for American ideas to take to market."

The game plan of the lobbyists for the foreigners and multinationals is to use the newly created corporation, with a board dominated by big-corporation types, to accomplish the same goal through regulations that never go through Congress.

Last year, FDA Week exposed that Patent Commissioner Bruce Lehman had made a deal to give the Chinese the entire U.S. patent data base on magnetic tapes, including five and a half trillion characters of information with technical drawings and chemical formulations.

Americans have to pay to get this data, but Lehman wanted to give this multi-million-dollar American asset free to the Chinese.

Senator Bond says that S. 507's changes in our patent system would have "enormous consequences." Indeed, they would. The consequences are all bad, and S. 507 has no redeeming value.

Chapter 7
Nobel Laurates Denounce Hatch's Patent Bill
October 1997

P resident Clinton's Council on Sustainable Development, whose chief current goal is to promote public acceptance of the Climate Change Treaty that Clinton will sign in December in Kyoto, is attempting to kill two birds with one stone by linking the treaty to Orrin Hatch's Omnibus Patent bill, S. 507. The link is "international harmonization of intellectual property rights," which the Clinton Administration is pursuing through Congressional bills, trade agreements, treaties, and outright giveaways.

The problem with "harmonization" of U.S. patent rights is that the Clinton Administration wants to harmonize on the basis of unsuccessful foreign patent systems, instead of the supremely successful American system.

Senator Hatch's Omnibus Patent bill was blasted recently at a national news conference in Boston by a distinguished group of 26 Nobel Laureates in economics, physics, chemistry and medicine. Remarkably, the signers of this joint statement include lifelong antagonists Milton Friedman and Paul Samuelson.

These luminaries released an open letter to the U.S. Senate that began unequivocally: "We urge the Senate to oppose the passage of the pending U.S. Senate Bill 507." Their reason? "It will prove very damaging to American small inventors and thereby discourage the flow of new inventions that have contributed so much to America's superior performance in the advancement of science and technology."

If anybody understands the importance of innovation and creativity to the unparalleled American achievements, it is the Nobel Laureates. And they stated flatly that "S. 507 could result in lasting harm to the United States and the world."

Their letter praised the "wonderful institution that is represented by the American patent system established in the Constitution in 1787, which is based on the principle that the inventor is given complete protection for a limited length of time, after which the patent ... becomes in the public domain, and can be used by anyone, under competitive conditions for the benefit of all final users."

The Nobel Laureates' letter brought out on the table the fact that S.507 toadies to the "large multinational corporations" at the expense of the constitutional rights of independent inventors. Indeed, the chief advocates of S.507 are the well-heeled lobbyists for the multinationals who look upon independent inventors working in their garages or bicycle shops as nuisances they would rather not deal with.

The Nobel Laureates' letter accurately defines our unique American patent system as "a delicate structure" which "should not be subject to frequent modifications." The letter added that "Congress, before embarking on a revision of our time-tested patent system, should hold extensive hearings on whether there are serious flaws in the present system that need to be addressed and, if so, how best to deal with them."

According to Dr. Dudley Herschback, 1986 Laureate in chemistry, S.507 "would create total chaos and of course it is conducive to fraud and deceit. This is a piracy bill." Dr. Franco Modigliani, 1985 winner of the Economics Nobel prize, emphasized, "It is against the spirit of the U.S. patent system which is a great economic and cultural invention."

Congressman Dana Rohrabacher (R-CA), the chief opponent of patent-law revision in the House, has received letters from foreign inventors who plead with America not to "harmonize" our system by adopting the patent system of other countries. Foreign inventors know only too well that the patent systems of most foreign countries are rigged in favor of powerful vested interests and the politically well-connected and against independent inventors.

Our Founding Fathers created the constitutional right of inventors to the "exclusive" ownership of their creations as a democratic right, available to every individual. This uniquely American system is responsible for the fact that the United States has produced 95 percent of the world's inventions.

But envious foreigners want to steal American inventions. The basic terms of S.507 were hatched in a deal in 1994 between the late Secretary of Commerce Ron Brown and the Japanese Ambassador.

It is noteworthy that S.507's sponsor, Orrin Hatch, is pushing another proposal to extend the term of songwriters' copyright protection from 50 to 70 years beyond the author's life. Hatch has a personal interest in that bill; he holds the copyright on a compact disc of religious songs he wrote.

So, Senator Hatch wants to protect the property rights of songwriters for 70 years but strip away the rights of inventors only 18 months after their patent applications are filed, whether or not the patent is ever granted!

Senator Hatch has tried to mollify critics of S.507 by amending it, but the bill is so bad that no amendments can make it acceptable. S.507 would open up all existing patents to reexamination, and it would put the Patent Office under a board of directors dominated by representatives of the multinational corporations.

Senator Hatch needs to be told that inventors' creations are entitled to at least as much protection as songwriters'.

Chapter 8
The Ominous Attack on American Inventors
March 1998

The high-priced lobbyists for the big multinationals are crawling all over Capitol Hill this month to urge passage of Senator Orrin Hatch's bill, S.507. It is called the Omnibus Patent bill, but it ought to be called the Ominous Patent bill because it would take away the traditional rights of American inventors in order to accommodate the multinationals and their foreign trading partners.

This is a classic battle of giant U.S. corporations versus the little guys. In this case, the little guys are the independent inventors, who are the mainspring of American progress and prosperity, plus the small businessmen, who are the source of nearly all the new jobs that are created.

S.507 was slightly amended before it came out of Hatch's Judiciary Committee, as was its companion bill H.R.400 before it passed the House last year, but both bills are so totally bad that they cannot be amended to make them acceptable. The bills' proponents arrogantly continue to argue for the original purposes of the bills, stating their intent to achieve them either by restoring the deleted sections or by implementing them afterwards by bureaucratic fiat.

At stake in S.507 is one of our most important constitutional rights: the right of inventors to have, for limited times, "the exclusive right to their ... discoveries," thus giving the inventor the time to perfect his invention and raise the resources to market it. This powerful incentive is unique to America and is the chief reason why America has produced ten times as many significant inventions as the rest of the world combined.

Under our highly successful system, when the inventor applies for a patent, his application is held in total secrecy by the U.S. Patent Office until the patent is issued. The patent then gives the inventor the legal safeguard to protect his invention against those who want to steal it or infringe it.

Publication of an inventor's application before the patent is issued would serve the financial interests of the multinational corporations, who could use their enormous resources to bully the independent inventor into making a cheap deal, or to invalidate his patent application, or to steal his idea and beat him into production.

The Japanese, who don't invent anything but are mighty clever copycats, have been trying for years to break our system. They have been demanding that all the details of every invention be made public 18 months after the application is filed, regardless of whether or not a patent is ever issued.

The American and Japanese systems are very different. Japan's economy is based on a partnership between government and the big corporations, and the Japanese patent system operates to make sure that industry controls and uses new innovations.

The U.S. system, on the other hand, favors private property, individual innovation and ingenuity, and an open door of opportunity for entrepreneurs. Our patent system is the centerpiece of this system and is designed to protect the rights of the individual inventors.

S. 507 is a disgraceful attempt to codify a backroom deal made by then-Secretary of Commerce Ron Brown on August 16, 1994 with Japanese Ambassador Takakazu Kuriyama promising that our patent law would be changed to acquiesce in the Japanese demands. Nobody denied this paper trail in the two days of House debate last year.

S. 507 also includes another Japanese demand, a change in our reexamination process. The bill would allow outside parties, both foreign and domestic, to challenge all existing U.S. patents.

The main, indeed the only, argument for S. 507 is that we should "harmonize" our patent system with the rest of the world, but that's a false description of this bill. It does nothing to get U.S. patents recognized worldwide; instead, it just diminishes the rights of U.S. inventors.

The text of S. 507 makes clear why the multinational corporations are lobbying so intensely for S. 507. It would transform the U.S. Patent Office into a private corporation, whose agents are guaranteed positions on the board of directors.

Patent Commissioner Bruce Lehman is lobbying for S.507 because the private corporation status would facilitate plans to build a $1.3 billion Patent and Trademark Office headquarters in Virginia so lavish that it has been dubbed the PTO Taj Mahal. Lehman has shown his disdain for independent inventors by calling them "weekend hobbyists."

Some might think that the importance of independent inventors has diminished because of the large research labs of multinational corporations. But a Harvard study in the 1960s found that, of 703 innovations introduced after 1945, only 133 came out of the laboratories of big corporations.

Another study in 1970 of 61 of the most significant 20th century inventions found that half of the inventions had been produced by individuals. Business consultant Paul Herbig states in his 1994 book, The Innovation Matrix, that independent inventors tend to make the most radical innovations in technology because they are not held back by corporate groupthink.

Senator Kit Bond (R-MO) will hold a Small Business Committee hearing on March 31 to hear from some of the inventors and Nobel Laureates who oppose S.507 and were excluded from the one brief hearing held by Orrin Hatch.

Chapter 9
Copyrights vs. the Public Interest
May 1998

ill Clinton got a big laugh when he joked at the White House Correspondents' Dinner that the 105th Congress is, like Seinfeld, about "nothing." But that's not true: Congress is trying to pass some very detrimental laws in some areas where we wish it were doing nothing.

Several pending bills to change our Copyright law illustrate two very unfortunate trends: creating more federal crimes, thereby widening the jurisdiction of federal courts, and tilting laws to favor big entrenched interests and multinational corporations.

H.R. 2589, which has already passed the House, would extend copyright protection for authors and songwriters for an additional 20 years beyond the present law. This is contrary to the spirit and intent of the U.S. Constitution, which assures authors and inventors the "exclusive" property right in their writings and discoveries "for limited times," after which the writing or invention becomes the property of the general public to enjoy.

The public has the right to use the writings and music of works whose "limited times" have expired. There is no good reason for the descendants of James Madison or Julia Ward Howe to receive royalties on the Federalist Papers or the Battle Hymn of the Republic.

The original 1790 copyright law set the limited time for copyrights at 14 years plus one 14-year renewal. The limited time period has been repeatedly extended until now it runs for the life of the author or artist plus 50 years, and 75 years for a corporation.

Powerful special interests now want to extend the time period to 70 years beyond the life of the author, and 95 years for corporations. Leading the charge are the Walt Disney Company, the American Society of Composers, Authors and Publishers (ASCAP), and the Gershwin Family Trust.

They want to keep Mickey Mouse and Porgy and Bess from moving into the public domain. But Disney himself borrowed freely from characters and stories that had been created by others in pre-copyright years and centuries, and future artists should be able to do likewise.

Walt Disney and George Gershwin have already enjoyed their exclusive property right far longer than intended by our original constitutional design. It is long overdue for their creations to go into the public domain as a part of our American culture to be enjoyed and used by all.

H.R. 2589 is so overreaching that, if it had been in effect earlier, everyone who used the pictures of Uncle Sam or Santa Claus during most of the 20th century would have had to pay royalties to the remote descendants of the 19th century cartoonist Thomas Nast.

ASCAP is one of the most litigious lobbies in America today. In 1995, ASCAP tried to force the Girl Scouts to pay royalties for the songs they sing around their campfires, until a torrent of bad PR forced retreat.

Last year, Congress passed the No Electronic Theft (NET) law, which provides very stiff federal prison terms for petty and non-commercial copyright infringements and practices long considered fair use. Previously, copyright infringement was a civil matter. Now, if you download unlicensed material worth over $1,000 within six months, you are guilty of a federal felony.

This law applies even if you did not pursue economic gain and did not redistribute what you downloaded. It's difficult to browse the internet without violating it, and there would probably be millions of felons if this law were strictly enforced.

Another bill, H.R. 2281, which is now pending in the House, attempts to expand NET by making it a crime to "circumvent a technological protection measure that effectively controls access to a work."

That artful phrase is designed to ban a variety of practices that have long been considered legitimate and have been upheld by the courts as "fair use" of copyrighted materials. For starters, we would lose our right to tape television programs for non-commercial use because all the new digital VCR machines would be forced to honor Hollywood's copy-protection schemes.

The bill would also outlaw reverse engineering, without which "you couldn't make applications that run on Windows," said Skip Lockwood, coordinator of the Digital Future

Coalition. "The products couldn't be produced by anybody else but Microsoft if it weren't for reverse engineering."

Although the Senate Judiciary Committee exempted reverse engineering when it took up a similar bill last week, Jack Krumholtz, Microsoft's director of government affairs, said, "We support the bill as it's [originally] written." Then he added, "This provision doesn't in any way change the existing balance between fair use and the rights of the copyright holder."

That's funny: the law does nothing, but Microsoft is very much in favor of it. Most observers agree that Microsoft and Hollywood would be the major beneficiaries of H.R. 2281, which imposes a penalty of up to five years in prison and up to $500,000 in fines, as well as civil damages.

Does it strike you as curious that the same Congressmen are sponsors of the Copyright bill to extend copyrights to 95 years, and of the Patent bill (S. 507) to cut off inventors' legal protection at 18 months? What those two ostensibly inconsistent bills have in common is that they both would benefit entrenched corporations at the expense of the innovators of the future and the public.

Chapter 10

Why Is Congress Criminalizing Copyright Law?

June 1998

A new plan to straitjacket the American public by criminalizing a common American practice is hidden in the WIPO Copyright Treaties Implementation Act. Powerful Hollywood and software corporations that are afraid of losing money from high-tech competition are behind this dramatic change in copyright law.

Senator Orrin Hatch rushed this bill through the Senate on May 14 as S. 2037 with almost no debate and on a voice vote of 99-0. Now called R.R. 2281, the plan is to pass it before the public realizes it.

R.R. 2281 makes it a felony, punishable by up to five years in prison and a fine of up to $500,000, to copy materials against the wishes of Hollywood and the software industries. That's for the first offense; any subsequent offense brings a prison term of up to ten years and a fine of up to $1,000,000.

The dangerous felons whom the politicians want to put behind bars are ordinary Americans who want to record and edit a television program or movie on their own VCRs in their own homes, a practice that is now perfectly legal. People do this, for example, when they go to the ballgame and want to tape a favorite sitcom to view later (even, perhaps, editing it by fast-forwarding through the commercials).

When VCRs first came into popular use, movie and television producers fought all the way to the U.S. Supreme Court to prevent consumers from taping programs and lost in Sony v. Universal City Studios (1984). The Court ruled that this is "fair use," assuming, of course, that you are not making a business of selling the copyrighted programs you record.

The television and movie producers reconciled themselves to this, knowing that homemade tapes would be inferior in quality to the original. Home VCRs proved to be extremely profitable to the movie industry, anyway, through home rentals.

Technology is changing rapidly, and, in a few years, television expects to move into the digital age. We will all have to buy new TV sets, and the quality of what we see on our screens will be, they say, remarkably superior to what we have today on our television sets. When you tape digital television programs, the copies will be just as good quality as the original. So, Hollywood, television producers and cable companies want to prevent consumers from all copying.

Heretofore, noncommercial copyright infringement has been a civil matter. That means, a copyright owner who thinks his property right has been infringed can sue for damages from the infringer.

Now, however, Hollywood and the software corporations have so much political clout that they are trying to make the government do their work for them. R.R. 2281 would convert current "fair use" of VCRs into copyright infringement, and convert noncommercial copyright infringement into a criminal offense, sending infringers to prison instead of just making them pay damages.

When something becomes a federal felony, that brings into action the U.S. attorney, the FBI, sting operations, and wiretapping, all at the expense of the taxpayers rather than the powerful corporations that claim to be injured. We have enough real crime to worry about and shouldn't use federal prosecutors to work for Hollywood.

Section 1201(a) spells out this new federal crime: "No person shall circumvent a technological protection measure that effectively controls access to a work protected under this title."

Hollywood and television producers plan to install "a technological protection measure" in their movies and programs, and then get government prosecutors to send to prison anyone who tries to "circumvent" it, as well as any VCR company that sells a VCR that might enable consumers to "circumvent" it.

H.R. 2281 also makes any editing of certain information at the beginning or end of a movie a crime if it is "without the authority of the copyright owner." The TV-watcher need not even intend to do such editing to be liable if a court finds that he had "reasonable grounds to know" that it constituted a violation of the act.

Adding insult to injury, the Senate exempted broadcasters from the act, so they can avoid these draconian penalties. Why should broadcasters get special privileges denied to the American public?

An alternate to H.R. 2281 is H.R. 3048, which has 47 sponsors. It includes civil penalties for copyright infringement rather than the criminal penalties in the Senate Hatch bill.

Congress seems intent on changing all our intellectual property laws to benefit big corporations. Another piece of copyright mischief, H.R. 2652, passed the House in May and is pending in the Senate. H.R. 2652 would reverse the 1991 Supreme Court ruling in Feist v. Rural Telephone Service that the telephone book white pages are not copyrightable. Copyrights are supposed to protect original and creative works, not compilations of public information.

Under H.R. 2652, databases of public domain information would be protected (no originality would be required), there would be no time limit on copyrights, and there would be no "fair use" exception. Even private, noncommercial extraction of information from a database would be punishable by five years in prison, and damages in civil lawsuits would be broadened.

It's time to call a halt to the peculiar passion of the Republican Congress to increase the jurisdiction of the federal courts by creating more and more new federal crimes, at the public's expense.

Chapter 11
Big Brother is Monitoring Us by Databases
September 1998

T he hottest issue in America today is our discovery that the Federal Government is trying to tag, track and monitor our health care records through national databases and personal identification numbers. This is a priority election issue, and every Congressional and Senatorial candidate should be ready to answer questions from his constituents.

Americans are accustomed to enjoying the freedom to go about our daily lives without telling government what we are doing. The idea of having Big Brother monitor our life and activities, as forecast in George Orwell's great book *1984*, is not acceptable in America.

Unfortunately, the liberals, who always seek control over how we live our lives and how we spend our money, are using terrorists, criminals, illegal aliens, welfare cheats, and deadbeat dads as excuses to impose oppressive government surveillance over our private lives. It is typical of the liberals to go after law-abiding citizens rather than just the law-violators.

Modern technology has made it possible to build a file on every American, and to record and track our comings and goings. Computers can now collect and store immense databases, with detailed records about individual Americans' health status and treatment, job status and applications, automobiles and driving, financial transactions, credit, banking, school and college performance, and travels within and without the country.

In the novel *1984*, an omnipresent Big Brother watched every citizen at home and work from a giant television screen. Databases can now accomplish the same surveillance and tracking much more efficiently. In the novel *1984*, Big Brother was able to read the individual's secret diary hidden in his home. The Clinton Administration and the FBI are right now demanding the right to read our email and computer files, listen in on our phone conversations, and track the whereabouts of our cell phone calls.

Some of these databases are under the direct control of the government (e.g., Internal Revenue, Social Security, and the Department of Education, which has amassed 15 national databases), and some are privately owned but give access to the government. These databases convey enormous power to whoever controls them. In government hands, they are the power to control our very life, our health care, our access to a job, our financial transactions, and our entry to school and college. In private hands, these databases are immensely profitable to the companies that own them and market them for commercial purposes.

The Clinton Administration, Congress, big corporations that funnel millions of dollars of soft money into political coffers, and some powerful foundations have cooperated in seeking federal legislation to establish a property right in these databases. So much power and money are involved in accessing and controlling personal information that the Washington lobbyists are moving rapidly to lock in the extraordinary powers Congress has already conferred on those who build databases and to build a wall of federal protection around them.

If we want to preserve American freedom, it's time to stop government access to these databases. Let's look at some of the ways that Clinton and Congress have cooperated in the building of databases that tag, track and monitor our daily lives.

1. The 1996 Kennedy-Kassebaum law (the Health Insurance Portability and Accountability Act) gives the Department of Health and Human Services (HHS) the power to create "unique health care identifiers" so that government can electronically tag, track and monitor every citizen's personal medical records. The plan is that everyone must submit an identification document with a unique number in order to receive health care, or the provider will not be paid. A database containing every American's medical records, identified by a unique number, was a central feature of Clinton's defeated 1994 health care bill, but it reemerged in the Kennedy-Kassebaum bill. Bill Clinton, Ted Kennedy, and Bob Dole all bragged about passing this law.

2. H.R. 4250, the 1998 Patient Protection Act, passed by the House on July 24, 1998, will allow anyone who maintains personal medical records to gather, exchange and distribute them. The only condition on distribution is that the information be used for "health care operations," which is vague and meaningless.

Even worse, H.R. 4250 preempts state laws that currently protect patients from unauthorized distribution of their medical records. There are several exemptions to the gathering of information that reveal the liberal bias of the drafters of this bill. The bill exempts from the gathering of medical records any information about abortions performed on minors. That provision is a sure sign of the kind of control of health care that this bill opens up.

3. The Collections of Information Antipiracy Act (which originally had another number) was added (just before House passage) to **H.R. 2281**, the 1998 WIPO Copyright Treaties Implementation Act and the internet Copyright Infringement Liability Clarification Act. No one, of course, is in favor of "piracy," but this bill goes far beyond any reasonable definition of piracy. This Collections of Information bill, in effect, creates a new federal property right to own, manage and control personal information about you, including your name, address, telephone number, medical records, and "any other intangible material capable of being collected and organized in a systematic way." This bill provides a powerful incentive for corporations to build nationwide databases of the personal medical information envisioned by the Kennedy-

Kassebaum law and the Patient Protection bill. This bill will encourage health care corporations to assign a unique national health identifier to each patient. The government can then simply agree to use a privately-assigned national identifier, and Clinton's longtime goal of government control of health care will be achieved.

Under the Collections of Information bill, any information about you can be owned and controlled by others under protection of Federal law. Your medical chart detailing your visits to your doctor, for example, would suddenly become the federally protected property of other persons or corporations, and their rights would be protected by Federal police power. This bill creates a new Federal crime that penalizes a first offense by a fine of up to $250,000 or imprisonment for up to five years, or both, for interfering with this new property right. It even authorizes Federal judges to order seizure of property before a finding of wrongdoing.

H.R. 2281 grants these new Federal rights only to private databases and pretends to exclude the government's own efforts to collect information about citizens. But a loophole in the bill permits private firms to share their federally protected data with the government so long as the information is not collected under a specific government agency or license agreement. This loophole will encourage corporations, foundations, Washington insiders and political donors to build massive databases of citizens' medical and other personal records, and then share that data with the government.

4. The 1993 Comprehensive Child Immunization Act authorized the Department of Health and Human Services "to establish state registry systems to monitor the immunization status of all children." HHS and the Robert Wood Johnson Foundation have since sent hundreds of millions of dollars to states to set up these databases (often without parental knowledge or consent).

The Centers for Disease Control (CDC) is aggressively trying to convert these state databases into a national database of all children's medical records. The CDC is using the tracking of immunizations as a ruse to build a national patient information system. The government is already demanding that all newborns and all children who enter school be given the controversial Hepatitis B vaccine. This is just the start of government control of our health care made possible by databases of medical records.

5. The 1996 Illegal Immigration Reform and Immigrant Responsibility Act (especially Section 656(b)) prohibits the use of state driver's licenses after Oct. 1, 2000 unless they contain Social Security numbers as the unique numeric identifier "that can be read visually or by electronic means." The act requires all driver's licenses to conform to regulations promulgated by the Secretary of Transportation, and it is clearly an attempt to convert driver's licenses into national I.D. Cards. This law also orders the Transportation Department to engage in "consultation" with the American Association of Motor Vehicle Administrators, which has long urged using driver's licenses, with Social Security numbers and digital fingerprinting, as a de facto national ID card that would enable the government to track everyone's movements throughout North America.

When Social Security was started, the government made a contract with the American people that the Social Security number would never be used for identification. Call this another broken promise.

Meanwhile, many states are already trying to legislate driver's licenses that are actually a "smart card" with a magnetic strip that contains a digitized fingerprint, retina scan,

DNA print, voice print, or other biometric identifiers. These smart cards will leave an electronic trail every time you use it. New Jersey's proposed smart card would even track your payment of bridge and highway tolls and loans of books from the library, as well as credit card purchases and visits to your doctor.

6. The 1996 Welfare Reform Act (the Personal Responsibility and Work Opportunity Reform Act) sets up the Directory of New Hires. All employers are now required to send the government the name, address and Social Security number of every new worker and every employee who is promoted. This will eventually be a massive database, tracking nearly every worker in America.

7. Public-private partnerships. An example of how databases and copyrights, in partnerships with the government, can be used for private gain and control over millions of people is the way the American Medical Association (AMA) worked out an exclusive contract with the Health Care Financing Administration (HCFA), a division of the Department of Health and Human Services (HHS). The AMA developed and copyrighted a database of 6,000 medical procedures and treatments to use as a billing system. The AMA then contracted with HCFA to force-the entire-health care industry (including all doctors) to buy and use the AMA's system.

A federal Court of Appeals reviewed this peculiar AMA/HCFA arrangement and, in August 1997, held that the AMA had "misused its copyright by licensing the [payment coding system] to HCFA in exchange for HCFA's agreement not to use a competing coding system." The court stated, "The plain language of the AMA's licensing agreement requires HCFA to use the AMA's copyrighted coding system and prohibits HCFA from using any other."

This exclusive government-granted monopoly is worth tens of millions of dollars annually to the AMA, and it ensures the AMA's support of any Clinton health care proposal, no matter how socialistic. This type of public-private partnership, often concealed from public scrutiny, is becoming the preferred technique to advance the liberal agenda.

The American people do not want their private life and activities monitored by Big Brother. Tell your Congressman and Senator to repeal all these provisions which protect the building of databases that track our daily activities.

'Rethinking' the Internet

When asked by reporters whether she favors curbs on the internet, which has played a key role in breaking the news about the President's scandals, Hillary Clinton ominously replied, "We are all going to have to rethink how we deal with this, because there are all these competing values." According to a Reuters dispatch, she went on to deplore the fact that the internet lacks "any kind of editing function or gatekeeping function." The now famous appearance of Matt Drudge at the National Press Club showed that Mrs. Clinton is not alone in attacking the notion that a website, such as the Drudge Report, without any supervisory editor, can compete with established news sources.

The copyright bill now racing through Congress, H.R. 2281, appears to emanate out of the mindset that we should rethink our laws about freedom of the internet. This is the same bill to which the Collections of Information Act (referred to in #3 above) was attached, and the other sections of the bill are just as ominous.

H.R. 2281, the WIPO Copyright Treaties Implementation Act and the Internet Copyright Infringement Liability Clarification Act, would significantly change U.S. copyright law at the behest of the big corporations. Copyrights are, of course, a good thing. But the lobbyists for Hollywood, cable, software and publishing industries are exploiting temporary confusion on Capitol Hill over high-tech issues.

H.R. 2281 has many provisions that are unacceptable in a free society. It sets up a procedure that effectively turns internet service providers into gatekeepers. A competitor asserting that you are infringing his copyright, can demand that your service provider delete your website, file or link. H.R. 2281 makes it almost sure that your service provider will punch the Delete button, no matter how insubstantial or frivolous the complaint, because the bill promises that "a service provider shall not be liable for monetary relief ... for infringement ... if the provider ... responds expeditiously to remove or disable the reference or link upon notification of claimed infringement."

It doesn't take a rocket scientist to figure out that, when a service provider receives an intimidating letter on legal letterhead demanding X, and he knows that if he expeditiously does X he is immune from a lawsuit, most service providers will do X. And presto, your website, file or link—the private property of the future—is taken from you without due process.

H.R. 2281 enables a bully (a corporation or special interest lobby) to eliminate future Drudges and others by merely intimidating the internet service provider. Neither a court order nor even a registered copyright is necessary for a competitor to demand removal of material from the internet.

The advocates of H.R. 2281 assert that the bill is designed to prohibit "black box" descramblers for cable TV, but the language of the bill goes far beyond this excuse. The bill will allow seizure of your computer or VCR without advance notice and without any finding of wrongdoing. This bill imposes prison sentences of up to five years if a Federal court determines that you were using a computer, VCR or website contrary to the rights of a copyright owner. H.R. 2281 empowers a Federal judge to order the seizure of your personal computer or VCR without any finding of wrongdoing. A proposed change to allow for 72-hour advance notice was rejected, even though prior notice of a deprivation of property is a constitutional right of due process. It could take you years of litigation to get your computer returned, and meanwhile your business is ruined just because of an alleged copyright infringement. The bill provides for a replacement of seized property, but only under certain conditions and only after the damage has already been done.

Microsoft, Time Warner, Hollywood and the publishing industry, the chief backers of H.R. 2281, should be able to protect themselves against unauthorized users without new legislation. Big corporations should not be permitted to use Federal prosecutors and judges, spending taxpayer dollars, to defend corporate interests against competitors.

As Silicon Valley engineers know, the computer industry was developed by the use of reverse engineering of competitors' products for the purpose of copying interfaces and discovering unpatented features. The internet itself is built on widespread copying and unfettered competition, with enormous benefit to the public. H.R. 2281 includes an exemption for reverse engineering, but it is limited to having a "sole purpose" of engineering "necessary"' for interoperability. That is so narrow that it is almost meaningless, and a competitor faces five years in jail if the court disagrees about the necessity or if the engineer could have learned the same information through a different, perhaps costlier, means.

Congress will be making an enormous mistake if it empowers Federal judges and gatekeepers to control the internet.

Hang Up on the Gore Phone Tax

Vice President Al Gore has staked his political reputation on allying himself with radical environmentalism and government manipulation of the internet. His schemes usually involve higher and hidden taxes, oppressive federal or even global regulations, and payoffs to political pals.

The Gore phone tax involves all these elements and burdens everyone who uses a telephone. There are no exemptions, no deductions, no credits, no cap or floor, no way to escape the obnoxious Gore phone tax that is added to everyone's monthly long-distance phone bill. Of course, your phone bill must be paid monthly, or your service is cut off, an even more effective technique than demands from the IRS.

The proper name for the Gore phone tax is the "E- rate" for education rate. It came out of the 1996 Telecommunications Act, which requires telecommunications companies to provide the lowest possible rates to schools and libraries, and to subsidize their installation of internet connections and telecommunications services. It's been dubbed the Gore tax because the Vice President is a chief proponent of this telephone tax.

The Gore phone tax was initially planned to be levied secretly so that the public wouldn't be aware of paying it, and the FCC pressured phone companies not to disclose the tax to their customers. But competition for phone rates has gotten so intense that the phone companies are refusing to take the hit of raising their rates without identifying the federal mandate that forced the increase. AT&T has added a 93-cent charge to every residential monthly phone bill, while other long-distance carriers have added a 5 percent charge.

The Gore tax is being challenged both in court and in Congress on the constitutional ground that the FCC has no authority to impose a tax, the taxing power being in the exclusive domain of Congress. Supporters of the tax say, "no problem; just call it a fee."

This Gore tax on every phone customer has already started producing a billion dollars in new federal tax receipts. The public school administrators and consultants know a cash cow when they see one. They are now engaged in a grant-writing frenzy and have already submitted 30,000 grant applications requesting more than $2 billion, much of it for school services only distantly related to internet connections. Most schools are already internet connected anyway. Reacting to political pressure, the FCC reduced the 18-month budget for the internet program from $3.35 billion to $1.9 billion. Schools have not received any money yet. This tax-and-spend boondoggle was slated to pay a salary of $200,000 to a Gore fundraiser, Ira Fishman. Congress reacted to this revelation by reducing his tax-paid salary to "only" $151,000, and Fishman subsequently resigned, citing "personal reasons."

When the government imposes more taxes, the public loses at both ends. It costs our hard-earned money when the tax is collected, and it does all kinds of mischief when the bureaucrats spend it. Letting the feds finance the internet connection to all public schools is an efficient means of controlling the curriculum, a major objective of the Clinton-Gore Administration. Of course, none of these new tax revenues will go to teach schoolchildren the basics. Students are not going to learn reading, writing and arithmetic by surfing the internet.

Ever since the landslide repudiation of Big Government in 1994, politicians have been afraid to raise taxes again. The

Gore tax (like the tobacco tax) is just another way to raise taxes but call it by another name.

Chapter 12
A Case Study on How a Bill
Passed the 105th Congress
December 1998

D o you sometimes wonder why bills that create a financial windfall to narrow special interests slide easily through the intricate legislative process, while bills that benefit the general public seem to get bogged down? Here is a case lesson in how this happens: Congressional passage of the Copyright Term Extension Act, a bill to extend copyright protection for authors and songwriters for an additional 20 years beyond current law.

The chief special interest promoting this bill was the Walt Disney Company because its copyright on Mickey Mouse was scheduled to expire in 2003, on Pluto in 2005, on Goofy in 2007, and on Donald Duck in 2009. Extending the copyright for 20 additional years is worth billions of dollars to the Disney Company.

As an author, of course I am very much in favor of copyright protection. But I also know that this precious constitutional right, enshrined in Article 1, is a property right that extends only, in the Constitution's words, "for limited times," after which the writing goes into the public domain for all to enjoy.

The framers of our Constitution set the "limited time" at 14 years plus one 14-year renewal. Congress has repeatedly extended the "limited time" until, at the start of this year, it ran for the life of the author or artist plus 50 years, and 75 years for a corporation. "Limited time" is not only a constitutional requirement, it is an excellent rule. There is no good reason for the remote descendants of James Madison, Julia Ward Howe, or Thomas Nast to receive royalties on the Federalist Papers, the Battle Hymn of the Republic, or Santa Claus.

No Disney family member is still connected with the company, which is now controlled by Michael Eisner, who had nothing to do with creating the Disney characters or building the enterprise. Not satisfied with the company's exclusive control for 75 years, Eisner set out to extend it to 95 years.

The Copyright Term Extension Act was introduced in 1997 by very key players: Senate Judiciary Committee

Chairman Orrin Hatch (R-UT) and House Judiciary Committee Intellectual Property Subcommittee Chairman Howard Coble (R-NC). The bill languished in the two Judiciary committees for months.

The Disney Political Action Committee (PAC) lined up Republican and Democratic cosponsors on the two Judiciary Committees and rewarded them with direct campaign contributions. Disney PAC cash contributions totaled $95,805 to Democratic Members of Congress and $53,807 to Republican Members, in addition to in kind contributions.

Of the 12 sponsors of the Senate bill, nine received contributions from Disney's PAC: Judiciary Committee Chairman Orrin Hatch (R-UT) (who received the largest contribution), Spencer Abraham (R-MI), Al D'Amato (R-NY), Mike DeWine (R-OH), Connie Mack (R-FL), and Robert Torricelli (D-NJ). The Disney PAC was particularly generous to Senate Minority Leader Tom Daschle (D-SD), and ranking Judiciary Democrat Patrick Leahy (D-VT) received $17,650 in personal contributions from Michael Eisner and 23 other Disney employees.

Eisner took his lobbying directly to Senate Majority Leader Trent Lott (R-MS). One week after they met, the

105

Disney PAC gave $1000 to Lott on the same day that he signed on as a co-sponsor.

Of the 13 sponsors of the House bill, ten received contributions from Disney's PAC: Subcommittee Chairman Howard Coble (R-NC) (who received the largest donation), Howard Berman (D-CA), Sonny Bono (R-CA), Charles Canady (R-FL), Chris Cannon (R-UT), John Conyers (D-MI), William Delahunt (D-MA), Elton Gallegly (R-CA), Bob Goodlatte (R-VA), and Bill McCollum (R-FL). The Disney PAC also contributed to Judiciary Committee Chairman Henry Hyde (R-IL).

Other special interests that stood to reap financial profits from this bill opened up their checkbooks, too. The Motion Picture Association PAC gave $43,232 to Republican and $34,000 to Democratic Members of Congress, benefiting most of the same Judiciary Committee members and copyright bill sponsors listed above, plus other sponsors Rick Boucher (D-VA) and Zoe Lofgren (D-CA).

Just as interesting as the money trail is the way the Republican and Democratic members of the two Judiciary Committees worked together to facilitate passage of this bill without hearings, debate, or notice to the public. The only hearing was held back in 1995 during the previous Congress, when it had been carefully managed to hear from those who stood to benefit financially.

If the bill ever had to face a floor debate, the "debate" would have been a sham because access to the floor was controlled in both Houses by ranking Republican and Democratic Judiciary Committee members, all of whom supported the bill. But the sponsors were skillful enough to avoid even a modicum of public debate.

On a single day, October 7, the Senate Judiciary Committee discharged the bill by unanimous consent, the full Senate passed the bill by unanimous consent (without a roll call), and the House passed the bill by voice vote under suspension of the rules. Clinton signed it on October 27 as Public Law 105-298.

The new book *Disney: The Mouse Betrayed* by Peter & Rochelle Schweizer proves conclusively that Eisner's Disney Company is the enemy of all the family values which Republicans cherish.

So, why did Judiciary Committee Republicans quietly put through legislation that hurts the public interest but is so immensely profitable to Disney?

Chapter 13
The Taj Mahal Could Be the
Tomb of Our Patent System
May 1999

T he elaborate marble mausoleum in India called the Taj Mahal, one of the world's most extravagant monuments, was built as the tomb of an emperor's favorite wife. The proposed new building complex to house the U.S. Patent and Trademark Office (PTO) has been tagged with the label Taj Mahal, not only because of its extravagant cost, but also because it threatens to become the tomb of America's unique patent system.

The price tag of $1.3 billion only buys a 20-year lease for an Alexandria, Virginia property; the PTO may have the option to buy it at market price at the end of that period. Funds for the lease will come from the patent fees paid by struggling inventors, that small group of individuals to whom we owe so much for creating the inventions that have made America the economic leader of the world.

The proposed PTO Taj Mahal is lavish beyond the dreams of any 17th century emperor in India. Furniture for the PTO's Taj Mahal is budgeted at $64 million, including $250 shower curtains, $750 baby cribs for daycare, $308 ash cans, and $1000 coat racks, according to a PTO-funded study.

There's more here than meets the eye. It's not just an excess of bureaucratic extravagance and the lust of former Patent Commissioner Bruce Lehman and Acting Patent Commissioner Q. Todd Dickinson to live in the luxurious style to which they would like to become accustomed.

The PTO Taj Mahal is part of a plan to radically change our unique American patent system by "corporatizing" it into what the Commerce Department's Inspector General calls a "Performance Based Organization." This means pretending that the PTO is a business that is selling products and modelling it after the multinationals that are lobbying aggressively for this change.

But the PTO is not a business; it is the guardian and facilitator of one of our most precious constitutional rights: the Article I, Section 8 inventors' "exclusive right" to their inventions "for limited times." The move to the proposed PTO Taj Mahal is part of an overall plan to change the PTO from a successful, free-from-fraud federal agency into a stand-alone, semi-private corporation, without essential public oversight of its activities.

Last year's patent bills (S. 507 and H.R. 400), which fortunately did not pass, would have created this pseudo-governmental corporation with guaranteed seats on the board of directors for representatives of the multinational corporations. The independent inventors, disdained by PTO Commissioner Lehman as "weekend hobbyists," would have been left out in the cold.

The multinationals are pushing hard for major changes in our patent law in order to "harmonize" U.S. patent law with foreign law, especially Japanese. But it's the unique American system that is responsible for the fact that more than 90 percent of inventions are American, and it makes no sense to harmonize down to unsuccessful foreign systems (which are skewed to corporate control instead of inventors' rights) instead of up to the successful U.S. system.

In March 1998, the Commerce Department's Inspector General reported that the Space Allocation Plan for the proposed PTO Taj Mahal contains no space for the paper search files, which are now the principal resource used by

110

patent examiners in granting new patents. Two centuries of paper records of American inventions, the greatest technical teaching library in the history of the world, will be banished, reducing us to total faith in electronic files.

The patent examiners are fighting hard to save the paper search files because they are more complete, more accurate, and contain thousands of original articles so essential to proving that new patent applications are for original work. Loss of these records will drastically diminish the examiners' ability to do an effective search.

In the new PTO building, public access will be restricted and the area of public search rooms will be reduced. All these curious facts indicate that the move to the Taj Mahal will not be merely a change in location or a modernization of facilities, but a drastic transformation of the function and purposes of the PTO in order to diminish the inventors' rights it is supposed to protect. .

There is no pressing need for a new building; current leases cost less and can run until 2014. Moving costs from current PTO offices in Arlington, Virginia are estimated at $5 million, but others claim it is closer to $130 million.

The constitutional property right of individual inventors is the mainspring of America's remarkable prosperity, high standard of living, and continual generation of new jobs and businesses. To borrow Winston Churchill's famous line, "Never in the field of human endeavor was so much owed by so many to so few."

That's why 25 Nobel Laureates joined together to oppose all patent legislation to "harmonize" our patent system with foreign systems and to corporatize the procedure. We hope Congress is listening.

Chapter 14
Who Controls Your Medical Records?
March 1999

We had hoped that the 106th Congress would address the health care and HMO issue by giving more power to patients. Instead, the House Subcommittee on Courts and Intellectual Property has scheduled a hearing this week on a bill to lay the groundwork for corporations to control, manipulate, and market our most intimate medical records.

Quietly introduced as H.R. 354, the Collections of Information Antipiracy Act, this dangerous legislation would grant a new federal right to corporations that build databases of patients' medical records. It would protect the corporations' control of these databases by threatening to prosecute anyone who interferes with this new right.

These new federal crimes carry penalties of a $250,000 fine and five years in jail for the first infringement, and twice that for the second. H.R. 354 would subject the mere copying of a part of a corporation's database to the jurisdiction of federal judges with the power to seize assets without a finding of guilt and impose huge fines and prison sentences.

This certainly wasn't what we had in mind when we heard politicians talk about "health care reform" or a "patient protection act." H.R. 354 is the product of behind-the-scenes deal making between a handful of powerful corporations and politicians.

The primary push for this bill comes from the American Medical Association (AMA), which is trying to get Congress to do a sidestep around a court decision the AMA lost in 1997 (Practice Management Info. Corp. v. AMA). At issue in that case was whether the AMA could control and charge fees for the sale of materials containing the Medicare codes that all health providers are required to use.

The marketing of databases is a very profitable part of the AMA's annual $230 million budget, since only a fourth of physicians are full dues-paying members and they provide less than a third of the AMA's revenue. In addition to its database of Medicare codes, the AMA has a database of all doctors, both members and nonmembers, stored with all sorts of personal and professional information.

Six months after the court held that the AMA had "misused" its rights in the Medicare code database, the AMA turned its powerful lobbying apparatus on Congress to arrange a legislative fix. The AMA testified that the purpose of this bill is "to protect collections of information, including databases such as ours," and then followed up with well-timed PAC contributions.

But Congress should not make "collections of information" a new federal right enforced by the police and judicial power of the federal government! The Supreme Court correctly ruled in Feist v. Rural Telephone Service (1991) that, under the U.S. Constitution, copyright protection is granted only to authors who create new works, not to corporations that merely collect data, and the phone companies do not own their listings of phone numbers just because they spent money collecting them.

H.R. 354 is deviously designed to finesse the Feist decision by creating a new federal right called "collections of information," and by giving a special exclusion to telephone listings (as well as for stock quotes and the news media), but not for medical records. The AMA testimony makes clear that the Collections of Information bill will create new rights not constitutionally available under copyright laws.

The Collections of Information bill failed to pass the Senate last year and, when the sponsor, Rep. Howard Coble (R-NC), reintroduced it as H.R. 354, he said that medical information is one of the focuses of the bill and that its purpose is to get around "recent cases." His subcommittee rejected attempts to exempt medical records from the sweeping new powers created by the bill.

Databases of personal information are a tremendous financial asset because they can be used for so many commercial purposes such as targeted marketing and health insurance underwriting. Since the health care database market is growing by a billion dollars a year, corporations already have ample incentives to build databases and make big money off of them, and they don't need Congress to legislate any new incentives.

Ambiguous language in H.R. 354 preempts state laws that currently ensure legitimate access by patients and physicians to their medical records. HMOs would be able to deny access, impose delays, or charge huge fees before providing essential medical records to patients or their physicians.

Most states have laws that guarantee patients the right to access their own medical records, but H.R. 354 would preempt these even though it exempts certain other state laws. H.R. 354 purports to exempt state privacy laws, but that exemption would be overridden by another bill expected to pass, the Patient Protection Act, H.R. 448.

By giving all these new rights in companies that build databases, H.R. 354 will make it difficult, expensive or impossible for individual Americans to access or restrict usage of their own personal information. We don't want the federal government to create new federal rights or incentives to encourage corporations to collect, manipulate, control, or market databases of medical records.

Chapter 15
Don't Fall for Phony Patent Reform
July 1999

Apple ll the bad deals made by the late Secretary of Commerce Ron Brown, unfortunately, did not die with him in his tragic plane crash. His deal to betray our unique American patent system, which we thought we killed in the 105th Congress, has been resurrected in the 106th.

Last year, it was called the Omnibus Patent Act, nicknamed the Ominous Patent Act. To make the sell-out palatable, the bill's sponsors rechristened it the American Inventors Protection Act, H.R. 1907, but it ought to be called the Inventor Elimination Act.

One has to ask, what powerful forces are so determined to change (in the phony name of "reform") our enormously successful patent system, the keystone of America's technological superiority and economic success? The answer is the suspect "partnership" fabricated between the Clinton

Administration and Japan and China, plus the multinationals whose god is globalism.

The unique American patent system, which was created by the writers of the U.S. Constitution and crafted by our nation's preeminent engineers George Washington and Thomas Jefferson, is the reason why America has produced more major inventions than all the rest of the world combined. They set up the U.S. Patent Office to protect the constitutional right of independent inventors to the "exclusive" ownership of their inventions for a limited number of years, after which the inventions belong to the public.

The American system, founded in freedom, gives every American the democratic opportunity to develop and own his invention, with that ownership protected by the government. Other countries are very different.

The Japanese system is based on collusion between the government and the big corporations, and the Chinese Communist system is based on military control of the economy. Those systems are very efficient in low-cost copying of American inventions, but they don't invent anything important.

The chief argument we hear in behalf of patent "reform" legislation is "harmonization." But why should America harmonize with unsuccessful systems? Let other countries harmonize with us!

Phony "reform" of the U.S. system is aggressively sought not only by the foreigners, whose motive is to steal U.S. intellectual property, but also by the multinationals that want to control all innovation and therefore look upon independent inventors as their natural enemies. If you are DaimlerChrysler or IBM, for example, you certainly don't want an independent inventor working in his garage to develop a new product that you don't control, and which might cut in on your market share. So, the lobbyists for patent "reform" have made some cosmetic changes in last year's Ominous Patent bill and reintroduced it as H.R. 1907. The bottom-line purpose remains the same, namely, to advantage the multinationals at the expense of independent inventors.

The essence of H.R. 1907 is to deliver control of the U.S. Patent Office, its policies and functions, to the big corporations. In the name of creating "an independent agency, separate from any department of the United States," the U.S. Patent Office would be changed from a government agency protecting independent inventors to a tool of the multinational corporations.

Title VI would make the U.S. Patent Office subject to "review" by a newly created "Patent Public Advisory Committee," which "shall include individuals with substantial background and achievement in finance, management, labor relations, and office automation." People with those resumes would be like foxes guarding the chicken coop.

The duties of this Public Advisory Committee are to "review the policies, goals, performance, budget, and user fees" of the Patent Office. And, this Committee must be "consulted" about any changes in the regulations.

The setting of patent policies, fees, and regulations is vitally important to America's independent inventors, and H.R. 1907 turns this over to control by the inventors' natural enemies. It makes no more sense to let big corporations (who are more likely to be infringers than innovators) have a voice in patent policies than to let organized crime review criminal law policy for the Justice Department.

Title II undermines the rights of independent inventors by providing for "prior user rights." This will enable corporations to claim a "prior use right" and thereby steal the independent inventor's constitutional right to "exclusive" ownership of his discovery.

Title V, which allows third parties to participate in an expanded reexamination process, gives infringers the opportunity to delay an inventor's effective use of his patent rights. Because it will encourage litigation, it should be called the "patent lawyers' full employment act."

The internet and advances in technology are facilitating the creation of brilliant inventions that compete against existing products—for the benefit of the public. The objective of many corporations, however, is to use their lobbyists and political contributions to induce Congress to enact legal protections for the status quo.

"Patent reform" is a code word for discouraging potential competitors by weakening the rights of independent inventors. All patent "reform" bills should be defeated if we care about America's future.

Chapter 16
Copyright Extremists Should
Not Control Information
January 2003

Copyright extremists are working to control as much information as possible. Almost every week we see a new example of how they are thwarting the free flow of information.

The leaders of the copyright lobby are the Hollywood movie distributors and the major music corporations known as music labels. The latter don't create any music; they just market and distribute CDs with music after they acquire control of the copyrights.

The major music labels operate through a lobbying organization called RIAA (Recording Industry Association of America) to maintain their monopolistic interests and stifle the online distribution of music. Its five largest members, which sell 85 percent of all CDs, were found by the Federal Trade

Commission in 2000 to have unlawfully kept the retail prices of CDs high.

The RIAA has pressured colleges into policing the computer networks used by their students. It has subpoenaed computer network providers in order to track people listening to music.

The U.S. Naval Academy seized 100 student computers suspected of containing unauthorized music and threatened the Annapolis midshipmen with court-martial and expulsion. These fine students are training to fight a war in behalf of our country, and they should be allowed to listen to a little music in their spare time.

The copyright extremists argue that essentially all downloaded music is illegal. They successfully lobbied Congress into extending copyright terms to life of the composer plus 70 years, and now they claim that copyright owners can dictate how, where and when people listen to music.

The U.S. Supreme Court is currently considering a challenge to the constitutionality of the latest copyright extension. Congress has extended the time period eleven times in the past 40 years.

All authority for copyright law comes from the U.S. Constitution, which states that the purpose of copyright protection is "to promote the progress of science and useful arts" and that copyright protection is granted only "for limited times."

The RIAA tried to put small radio station webcasters out of business while secretly giving National Public Radio affiliates a sweetheart deal not available to other radio stations. Only last-minute intervention by outgoing Senator Jesse Helms gave small radio stations the legislative right to play music while paying reasonable royalties.

A teenager is on trial in Norway for figuring out a novel way to play DVD movie discs on his personal computer. He should be commended for his ingenuity, not punished. Adobe (a U.S. computer software company) persuaded U.S. law enforcement to throw a visiting Russian scholar in jail after he revealed some shortcomings in an Adobe e-book product at a public conference in this country. He was eventually released on condition that he testify against his own company.

The company has just been acquitted in a jury trial. Adobe could not find any example of anyone using the Russian software improperly.

Major retailers are now using copyright law to try to stop websites from posting advance information about sales. It's understandable that retailers want to keep it secret that they might be cutting prices after a holiday, but that is not the purpose of copyright law.

Microsoft now uses its Windows license agreement to try to limit criticism by its customers. It says, "You may not disclose the results of any benchmark test of the .NET framework component of the OS Components to any third party without Microsoft's prior written approval ... All rights not expressly granted are reserved by Microsoft."

The CEO of Turner Broadcasting says that television viewers are guilty of "stealing" if they skip the commercials. She says, "Your contract with the network when you get the show is you're going to watch the spots."

Eight Hollywood studios have filed suit against local retailers who buy their videos and DVDs and then delete the nudity, violence and foul language for the benefit and at the expense of their customers. Hollywood doesn't lose any sales from this practice; Hollywood is just determined to force viewers to watch the lurid sex and violence.

Copyright extremists are committing all this mischief under current law. Yet, the music labels and Hollywood argue that current laws are not strong enough, and they are lobbying for an assortment of new anti-consumer legislation.

One proposal would allow them to vandalize computer networks that they believe might be transmitting unauthorized content. Another proposed bill would force computer equipment makers to rig their computers, so buyers can only see and hear what is authorized, and another proposal would give copyrights to privacy-invading databases.

The purpose of copyright law is to provide incentives and protection to authors to create and publish original works, not give corporations the power to control the flow of information. We should not permit copyright extremists to exploit current laws for that goal, and we should reject their demands that Congress give them even broader power to control and license information.

Chapter 17
Will Corporations Own Our Identities?
October 2003

No one should be able to own facts about other people. Our names and numbers, and also the laws we must obey, should not be property that can be owned by corporations and policed by federal courts.

But special interests, such as the Software and Information Industry Association, are seeking new powers to own facts about us and about information we need. After quietly shopping a bill to Members of Congress for several weeks, the Database and Collections of Information Misappropriation Act was finally introduced last week as H.R. 3261.

The Constitution authorizes Congress to create copyrights. But your name, address and telephone number are facts that cannot be copyrighted, as the Supreme Court said when it ruled in 1991 that no one can copyright the telephone book.

The Constitution authorizes copyright protection for "authors." The Court ruled in Feist v. Rural Tel. Serv. Co. that a collection of facts lacks sufficient creativity to constitute authorship.

H.R. 3261 doesn't use the word copyright, but it would create a new federal property right in online and offline databases (collections of information) and give the federal courts power to police the use of information in databases. Granting large U.S. and foreign corporations the power to own personal facts about individuals, and prevent others from using those facts, would be the most lucrative handout in years.

H.R. 3261 would allow federal courts to impose stiff penalties if someone uses information from a database that a corporation claims to own. The exceptions to this rule are vague and subject to contrary interpretations, leaving users liable to a lawsuit in which it's up to a federal judge to decide what is "reasonable."

Over the past decade, without federal legislation or judicial supervision, databases have grown rapidly in size and number, and today there are giant databases containing our travel plans, our medical records, our telephone calls, our credit card usage, and even the websites we visit.

This Collections of Information bill would chill productive activity because few users of data can afford taking a chance on how a court might rule.

Prominent groups from all across the political spectrum vigorously oppose this new bill. The U.S. Chamber of Commerce says that the legislation could even prevent people from using data found in books checked out of libraries.

Peter Veeck felt the brunt of the corporate police. When he posted on his website the municipal building safety codes that all are required to obey, he was sued by a company that claimed to own the building codes.

After long and costly litigation, in 2002 Veeck won the case called Veeck v. SBCCI.

Judge Edith Jones wrote for the Fifth Circuit en banc: "Citizens may reproduce copies of the law for many purposes, not only to guide their actions but to influence future legislation, educate their neighborhood association, or simply to amuse."

On the last day of the U.S. Supreme Court term in June, the Court let Veeck's victory stand. During the litigation to force Veeck to remove building safety codes from his website, a hundred people perished in the Rhode Island nightclub fire attributed to ignorance about building safety codes.

The special interests still want Congress to allow corporations to exercise exclusive ownership over collections of facts. They failed to pass a similar bill called the Collections of Information Anti-Piracy bill in 1998 and are now trying again with H.R. 3261 in order to get from Congress what they could not win in the courts.

The real gold may lie in the medical databases that are still largely secret. The next time you want an itemization of why a brief hospital stay costs you far more than the most luxurious hotel, remember that medical procedure codes and reimbursement rates are not freely published.

The American Medical Association (AMA) claims to own these federally required codes, reaping tens of millions of dollars in royalty fees from them. You can go on the internet and find the price of almost anything from a plane ticket to an automobile, but the AMA will sue anyone who dares to post the billing codes and rates for simple medical procedures.

Giving new powers to the federal courts to police the use and exchange of information collected in databases would have a negative effect on our already shaky economy. Creating federally mandated ownership over data is not the way to go if we still believe in free enterprise.

Nor is H.R. 3261 the way to go if we believe that the federal government should exercise only enumerated powers. The Constitution does not authorize Congress to create any property rights beyond those specified in the Copyright Clause.

Chapter 18
So-Called Patent Reform Cheats U.S. Inventors
June 2007

The globalists are making a new attempt to circumvent and weaken a right explicitly recognized in the U.S. Constitution: Americans' exclusive ownership of their own inventions. Fortunately, Senators Tom Coburn (R-OK), Charles Grassley (R-IA), Jon Kyl (R-AZ), Jeff Sessions (R-AL), and Sam Brownback (R-KS) have exposed this mischief and called on Judiciary Committee Chairman Patrick Leahy (D-VT) and Ranking Republican Arlen Specter (R-PA) to slow down and discuss the proposed legislation before making costly mistakes.

As we've learned with "Comprehensive Immigration Reform," we should all be on guard any time politicians patronize us with pompous talk about "reform." The so-called Patent Reform Act of 2007 is not reform at all; in one package, it betrays both individual rights and U.S. sovereignty.

It's no accident that the United States has produced the overwhelming majority of the world's great inventions. It's because the Founding Fathers invented the world's best patent system, which was a brilliant stroke of inspired originality when the Constitution was written in 1787, and still is stunningly unique in the world.

The political pressure for the new bill comes from the "world is flat" globalists who want to level the U.S. patent system with other countries. "Harmonization" is a favorite trigger word in their arguments.

For example, in introducing the new bill, Rep. Howard Berman (D-CA) said it will "harmonize U.S. patent law with the patent law of most other countries." The explanation of the bill issued by Senator Leahy's office states that the bill's purpose is to eliminate "a lack of international consistency."

But since the U.S. system produces more important inventions than the rest of the world combined, why should we legislate "consistency" with inferior foreign policies?

The uniqueness of the American system is that "inventors" are granted "the exclusive right" to their inventions "for limited times" (usually about 18 years) after which the invention goes into the public domain. Exclusivity was assured because our courts would uphold the inventor's patent against infringers, and the U.S. Patent Office would not disclose any information in a patent application unless and until the legal protection of a patent was granted. Rejected patent applications were returned to the applicants with their secrets intact.

The so-called patent "reform" of 1999 radically changed this to allow the U.S. Patent Office to publish the details of inventions 18 months after they are filed, unless the inventor agrees NOT to file a patent application in another country. Other countries do not respect inventors' rights granted by the U.S. Patent Office.

Inventors say the U.S. Patent Office is now taking an average of 31 months to grant a patent! So, when the Patent Office publishes (i.e., posts online) a patent application before a patent is granted, this gives patent pirates all over the world an average of 13 months (31 minus 18) to study detailed descriptions of virtually all U.S. patent applications, steal and adapt these new American ideas to their own purposes, and go into production.

Foreign governments, foreign corporations, and patent pirates are thus able to systematically "mine" U.S. patent applications and steal American-owned inventions. The 2007 "reform" bill's "harmonization" is a fraud because it does nothing to require or induce other countries to respect U.S. patents.

The unconscionable delay in processing patent applications resulted when Congress diverted the fees paid by inventors into pork and other pet projects. That meant the Patent Office could not hire the additional examiners it needed to process the rising number of domestic and foreign patent applications, and so a massive backload built up.

What recourse does the inventor have? If the infringer is in another country (China is a notorious thief of intellectual property), the U.S. inventor must have filed a patent application in that other country and the lawsuit must be filed there.

The proposed Patent Reform Act of 2007, sponsored by Senators Leahy (D-VT) and Orrin Hatch (R-UT) and Rep. Berman (D-CA) and Lamar Smith (R-TX), would further reduce inventors' rights. For the sake of "international consistency," it would convert the U.S. system to a "first to file" system, thereby replacing our unique and successful U.S. "first to invent" system.

The U.S. now gives priority to the first one who actually invents something rather than to one who simply files papers about what he plans to invent. The change to "first to file" would create a race to the Patent Office and would severely disadvantage the small and independent inventors who lack the resources of the big corporations.

Much more is wrong with the Patent Reform Act of 2007, but I've run out of space, so stay tuned.

Chapter 19

Economic Integration of Our Patent System

August 2007

In extraordinary Senate-House coordination, the two Judiciary committees in the same week in July voted out a bill (S.1145 and H.R.1908) which, if it becomes law, will spell the end of America's world leadership in innovation. Called the Patent Reform Act, it is a direct attack on the unique, successful American patent system created by the U.S. Constitution.

As we've learned with "comprehensive immigration reform," we should all be on guard any time politicians patronize us with pompous talk about "reform" or "comprehensive." The so-called Patent Reform Act of 2007 is not reform at all; in one package, it betrays both individual rights and U.S. sovereignty.

It's no accident that the United States has produced the overwhelming majority of the world's great inventions. It's because the Founding Fathers invented the world's best patent system, which was a brilliant stroke of inspired originality when the Constitution was written in 1787, and still is stunningly unique in the world.

The uniqueness of the American system is that "inventors" are granted "the exclusive right" to their inventions "for limited times" (usually about 18 years) after which the invention goes into the public domain. Exclusivity was assured because our courts would uphold the inventor's patent against infringers, and the U.S. Patent Office would not disclose any information in a patent application unless and until the legal protection of a patent was granted.

So, prior to 1999, the U.S. Patent Office was required to keep secret the contents of a patent application until a patent was granted, and to return the application in secret to the inventor if a patent was not granted. That protected the legal rights of the inventor, who could then go back to the drawing board to perfect his invention and try again.

A mischievous congressional "reform" in 1999 authorized the U.S. Patent Office to shift to the Japanese and European practice of publishing patent applications 18 months after filing whether or not a decision is yet made on granting a patent. "Publish" means posting online on the internet.

The U.S. Patent Office reports that it is now taking an average of 31 months to grant a patent! So, when the Patent Office publishes (i.e., posts online) a patent application before a patent is granted, this gives patent pirates all over the world an average of 13 months (31 minus 18) to study detailed descriptions of virtually all U.S. patent applications, to steal and adapt these new American ideas to their own purposes, and to go into production.

Foreign governments, foreign corporations, and patent pirates are thus able to systematically "mine" U.S. patent applications and steal American-owned inventions.

By 2006, the U.S. Patent Office had placed 1,271,000 patent applications on the internet, giving access to anyone anywhere in the world. This foolish practice created a gold mine for China, Russia and India to steal U.S. innovations and get to market quickly.

Chinese pirates don't roam the high seas looking for booty but sit at their computers, scan the internet, and steal the details of U.S. inventions that the U.S. Patent Office loads online. This practice has become China's R&D program, and it is even more efficient than China's network of industrial and military spies.

The unconscionable delay in processing patent applications resulted when Congress diverted the fees paid by inventors into pork and other pet projects. That meant the Patent Office could not hire the additional examiners it needed to process the rising number of domestic and foreign patent applications, and so a massive backload built up.

What recourse does the inventor have? The 1999 "reform" law allows a patent application to be exempt from the publication requirement if the inventor agrees not to file a patent application in another country. But the default procedure is to publish.

If the other country infringes on the U.S. inventor's rights, the U.S. inventor must file his lawsuit in that foreign country. Other countries do not respect inventors' rights granted by the U.S. Patent Office, and China is a notorious thief of U.S. intellectual property.

The 2007 Patent "Reform" bill would delete this exemption and require publication of all patent applications 18 months after filing even though a decision has not yet been made on granting a patent. The 2007 Patent "Reform" bill is a fraud because it does nothing to require or induce other countries to respect U.S. patents and because it makes U.S. inventors even more vulnerable to theft of their property.

U.S. policy has always been to grant a patent to the first one who actually invents something. But the proposed Patent "Reform" Act, sponsored by Senators Patrick Leahy (D-VT) and Orrin Hatch (R-UT) and Reps. Howard Berman (D-CA) and Lamar Smith (R-TX), would further reduce inventors' rights by replacing our unique and successful "first to invent" system with the foreign "first to file" system. The U.S. now gives priority to the first one who actually invents something rather than to the first to file papers. The change to "first to file" would create a race to the Patent Office and would severely disadvantage the small and independent inventors who lack the resources of the big corporations.

First-to-file would be a windfall to the mega-corporations. First-to-file would invite an avalanche of applications from the big companies that have the resources to grind out multiple filings, and the small inventor would be lost in the shuffle.

The new Patent "Reform" bill offers yet another way for patent pirates to steal our technology. It's called post-grant review: a plan to make it easier to challenge patents during the entire life of the patent.

Still another provision of the new Patent "Reform" bill would shift decision-making about damages for patent infringement in such a way that the patent holders would get virtually no payment from infringers. This provision would increase litigation and limit the ability of independent inventors and small companies to enforce their rights or to win just compensation from those who infringe their rights.

The new Patent "Reform" bill would also transfer unprecedented rule-making authority to the Patent office. That's an abdication of congressional responsibility. The inevitable result would be the politicizing of the Patent Office.

Add it all up, and it is clear that the new Patent "Reform" bill is a big attack on the constitutional property rights of individual inventors and small enterprises, the very kind of entrepreneurs who give us our most important innovations. About a third of all U.S.-origin patent applications are filed by individual inventors, small companies, universities, and non-profit groups.

The common thread in the changes to be made by the new Patent bill is that they favor big companies like Microsoft and hurt individual and small-entity inventors.

Microsoft has thousands of patents, and recently argued that the free GNU/Linux operating system infringes over 200 of them. Microsoft wants to be able to use its huge patent portfolio to intimidate potential competitors, and at the same time it wants it to be easier to knock out individual patents.

While the real goal of the Patent "Reform" bill is to advantage big corporations over small and small-entity inventors, the "world is flat" globalists hide behind the mantra of the alleged need for "harmonization" and "consistency" to level the U.S. patent system with other countries. In introducing the new bill, Rep. Berman said it will "harmonize U.S. patent law with the patent law of most other countries." The explanation of the bill issued by Senator Leahy's office states that the bill's purpose is to eliminate "a lack of international consistency."

But since the U.S. system produces more important inventions than the rest of the world combined, there is no reason to legislate "consistency" with inferior foreign policies.

If Congress wants to do something constructive for our patent system, Congress should reinstate the rule that the Patent Office may not publish a patent application until a patent is granted, and if it is denied the application must be returned to the inventor with his secrets intact.

Congress should also give back to the Patent Office the flow of fees paid by inventors, which Congress took away in 1999 to spend on other projects. Then the Patent Office can hire more examiners and reduce its backlog of 800,000 applications.

Congress should put trade penalties on Communist China until it stops its notorious business of stealing our intellectual property.

The U.S. patent system is the vital factor in the technological lead that gives us the edge over competitors and enemies. We must not let the globalists and the lobbyists for multinational corporations destroy it.

Chapter 20
The Patent Act Is a Cheat on Americans
October 2007

W hen displaced American workers complain about outsourcing U.S. manufacturing jobs to take advantage of cheap Chinese factory labor, and about insourcing low-paid Asians on H-lB visas to take engineering and computer jobs, the globalists and multinational corporations have a ready answer. They recite in chorus: don't worry, be happy, because American technology and innovation enable us to compete in the global market.

But now those same globalists and multinationals are trying to outsource our technology and innovation advantage by delivering a body-blow to our unique and original patent system. This plan comes under the deceptive label Patent "Reform" Act (H.R. 1908), and it's already been rushed through the U.S. House.

Our patent system is the reason why nearly all the world's great inventions are American, giving us a standard of living that is the envy of the world. The right of inventors, large and small, to own their own inventions, is so important that it (along with copyright) is the only "right" protected in the original U.S. Constitution (preceding all the more famous rights spelled out in constitutional amendments).

A combination of foreigners who make a business of stealing our intellectual property, and the multinationals who want to avoid paying royalties to small inventors, have ganged up to get Congress to do their bidding. The battle is going on behind closed doors between the corporations with richly-paid lobbyists vs. the small inventors and businesses who produce 40 percent of U.S. innovation.

This attempt to bully the small guys with legislation doesn't make sense. But it's rolling through the halls of Congress because it has dodged publicity.

Item #1: The Patent "Reform" Act would change the rule for granting patents from the American first-to-invent requirement to the foreign procedure called first-to-file. This provision is arguably unconstitutional: the U.S. Constitution protects the ownership "right" for "inventors," not filers.

There is no good reason to prefer any foreign procedure over the successful American system. And there is a mighty good reason not to: first-to-file would bring a tsunami of applications ground out by the multinationals' large staffs, leaving the small inventors buried in paper.

Item #2: The Act would make it mandatory for the U.S. Patent Office to publish (i.e., post on the internet) all inventions 18 months after date of application, thereby repealing the option now used by 37 percent of American inventors to prevent publication by agreeing not to file in foreign countries. The big winner of this nasty provision would be the Asian pirates who sit at their computers and steal American inventions between publication at 18 months and 32 months, which is the average time it takes for a patent to be granted.

Item #3: The Act would create post-grant review, a process that would enable patent infringers to challenge the validity of a patent after it is issued without going to court, thereby making the inventor's ownership vulnerable and reducing his ability to attract venture capital to produce it. The big winners would be the multinationals with lots of lawyers.

Item #4: The Act would reduce the damages that a judge and jury can award to an inventor after proof that his invention has been stolen or infringed. Again, the winners would be the multinationals with big legal departments and deep pockets.

Item #5: The Act would weaken protections under U.S. trade laws that prevent foreign pirates from exporting their products made with stolen intellectual property into the United States. The result would be a perverse incentive to export our technology and jobs to foreign countries.

The advocates of the Patent Act say that it is needed to reduce patent litigation. Au contraire: the bill is more likely to increase not reduce litigation, and the percentage of lawsuits has remained constant for the last 15 years at about only 1.5 percent of all patents granted.

In 2007, the Supreme Court and the Federal Circuit (which hears patent appeals) handed down several precedent-changing decisions about patents which appear to shift the balance of power away from independent inventors and small businesses. The Patent "Reform" Act was written before any of these important decisions, and we should wait and see their effect before rushing in with new legislation.

There are a couple of problems with our current patent process that need fixing, but the Patent Reform Act doesn't address those. Congress should restore to the U.S. Patent

Office the revenue from the fees paid by inventors with their applications, which Congress took away in 1999 in order to divert the money to federal spending projects.

With more revenue, the Patent Office could hire and train more qualified examiners so that patent applications could be processed within 18 months.

Americans cannot afford to get it wrong about protecting our patent system. It is crucial to maintaining our world leadership in technology and innovation.

Chapter 21
Death for Innovation
March 2011

T he Democratic Senate is itching to pass a bill that will mean death for innovation, which is the backbone of American economic growth. Senator Patrick Leahy's (D-VT) bill, S.23, is called patent reform, but it's not reform; it will kill innovation by litigation.

Now that the globalists have transferred millions of good American jobs to Asians willing to work for as little as 30 cents an hour with no benefits, all we have left to maintain and restore our economic wellbeing is our innovation superiority. The United States is the world leader in inventing useful and important products and processes, while other countries build their economies by copying our innovations.

The mainspring of our success is the American patent system, unique when the Founding Fathers put it into the U.S. Constitution even before freedom of speech and religion, and still unique today. Unfortunately, some globalists outside and even inside the United States want to reduce the American standard of living.

The core of our time-tested patent-granting system goes under the label first-to-invent, plus a one-year grace period. It is only common sense that the patent should be granted to the first person who actually invents something, and our Constitution specifically identifies "inventors" as the owner of the property right.

The one-year grace period allows an inventor time to experiment with his invention, perfect it, make sure it works, offer it for sale, perhaps begin commercialization, find funds to complete his work and apply for a patent, and seek partners and investors. This system is essential for the protection of individual inventors and small businesses.

Other countries are free to imitate our system, but foreign countries haven't copied our system. Instead, they want to copy our inventions, and they devise all sorts of tactics to cheat us. Their code word is harmonization; we are hammered with the agitprop that globalization requires us to harmonize our laws with the rest of the world (which does not include obligating foreigners to respect U.S. patents). It's a betrayal of American inventors to harmonize down to inferior foreign practices; we should encourage them to harmonize up to our proven system.

Leahy's bill would replace the first-to-invent plus grace period with first-to-file plus litigation. That would grant the patent to the first to file an application at the U.S. Patent Office, even if another person actually built the invention first. That change would create a paper race to the Patent Office, which already has a backlog of 700,000 applications. Advocates of the Senate bill claim this will facilitate deciding who is the real inventor.

However, that's not a problem with first-to-invent. Last year there were only 47 challenges out of 500,000 first-to-invent patent applications.

The core principle of our system is awarding the patent to the true inventor. It's wrong, and probably unconstitutional, to take that away for presumed administrative ease.

The Senate bill would also institute a European-style post-grant challenge process to invalidate the patent. In Europe, competitors use this process to tie up the patent in expensive administrative legal proceedings which independent inventors and small businesses can't afford.

Canada recently shifted to a first-to-file system and found that it imposed a special hardship on independent inventors, startups, and small businesses that don't have in-house lawyers or resources to hire expensive outside counsel.

The Leahy bill eliminates the grace period from offering an invention for sale or making public use of it, leaving only a grace period from "disclosure" of the invention. The bill does not define disclosure, so bring on the lawyers to litigate its meaning.

The value of first-to-invent over first-to-file was explained by inventor Steve Perlman, CEO of Reardon, OnLive and MOVA. He experimented with 100 inventions over five years of development, but only six were actually used and filed for patents.

He explained that a large part of invention is trying out a vast number of ideas, such as Edison with thousands of light bulb filaments and the Wright Brothers with many wing shapes. First-to-file means flooding the Patent Office with dead-end applications.

Another unfair and biased aspect of the Leahy bill is that not a single practicing inventor or representative of small

PHYLLIS SCHLAFLY SPEAKS, VOLUME 4

business was called to testify during five years of Senate hearings on patents.

The first-to-invent system has served us well. If it ain't broke, don't fix it.

Chapter 22
The Patent Act is Dangerous to U.S. Security
May 2011

Ore and more dangerous effects of the proposed changes to U.S. patent law (S.23, H.R.1249) keep emerging, especially since the hearings failed to hear from any real inventors. The proposed bill is unconstitutional, an attack on our national security, and an offense against the rule of law.

By awarding patents to the First-to-File an application with the bureaucracy instead of to the First-to-Invent, the proposed bill will deprive inventors of their constitutional property right set forth in Article I, Section 8. U.S. law has always awarded patents to real inventors, not to paper-pushers.

An important letter sent to House Speaker John Boehner (R-OH) from the 15-member Inventors Network of the Capital Area describes how the proposed patent bill "threatens all individual and corporate Research &

Development in America, the backbone of our national defense and economic security." Here is how this racket will work.

Inventors don't usually give birth to their inventions like the Greek goddess Athena, who was born fully grown and fully armed out of Zeus's head. The Wright Brothers required many experiments as they tried wings with different angles before they were ready to patent heavier-than-air flight.

The proposed patent bill will enable Chinese hackers to steal U.S. innovation secrets while they are in development, then file an application with the U.S. Patent Office under First-to-File, and thereby own new U.S. technology instead of merely stealing it. Owning the patents will enable China legally to take away ownership rights and profits from Americans who actually invent new technologies.

Defense technologies would be a prime target of this threat. The First-to-File provision of the Patent Act would become the most effective weapon in China's arsenal and would threaten our national security in a new and ominously dangerous way.

National security expert Adam Segal testified before the House Foreign Affairs Subcommittee on Oversight and Investigations about the dangers from Chinese cyber espionage, massive theft and piracy, and the policy called "indigenous innovation," which requires technology transfer in return for market access. He said, "it is clear that the United States must do more to defend itself."

Since 1870, U.S. law has provided a grace period of one year between the date the invention is disclosed and the date the patent application is submitted. This grace period gives an inventor a year to perfect his invention, to sort out better from inferior features, to raise capital, to gather partners, and to field test the invention before the deadline for filing a patent application.

This grace period is very important to independent inventors, small companies and startups. It permits them to delay the costs of filing until the invention is evaluated, a decision is made as to whether it is worth spending money on, and investment capital is raised.

The proposed bill redefines the grace period in a way that is hostile to small inventors and small businesses because it states that any disclosure of the invention by anyone other than the inventor at any time, even within that first year, will bar the real inventor from getting a patent. Weakening the grace period thus poses an enormous risk to the most innovative sectors of our economy.

Another outrage of the proposed patent bill is the provision that subjects to expensive new litigation and retroactively attacks the patent on the check-clearing system which enables banks to return photo images to their depositors rather than actual canceled checks. This new system saves the banks millions of dollars because they no longer have to truck the checks physically to other banks to be cleared.

This system was created by inventor Claudio Ballard, who received a patent for it, survived post-grant review, and won expensive court battles when he defended his patent against infringement by the banks. After all that, the new patent bill (ignoring the principle of res judicata—the thing is already decided) sets up an unprecedented procedure to overturn the patent office and court decisions, giving the banks another chance to invalidate Ballard's patent.

A 15-page letter to Congress from Prof. Richard A. Epstein, the nation's foremost authority on property rights, explains how the "stacked procedures of Section 18" in the bill are designed to let banks use Ballard's invention without paying him for it. Epstein, who wrote the book on "Takings" under the Fifth Amendment, says Ballard deserves just compensation for the use of his patent.

Altogether, the proposed bill, mischievously called "patent reform," is a bad, dangerous and dishonest bill that must be defeated if we care about respecting the Constitution, inventors' property rights, and American leadership in innovation.

Chapter 23
Unconstitutional Attack on American Inventors
June 2011

O ne of the most valuable individual rights guaranteed in the U.S. Constitution is the right of "inventors" to own " the exclusive right" to their "discoveries" for "limited times." This right was set forth in Article I, Section 8, years before the rights to freedom of speech and religion were added.

This right is recognized and reinforced by our system of granting patents to inventors, so they will be able to protect their exclusive ownership for a limited number of years, after which the invention goes into the public domain. U.S. patents are awarded to the "first-to-invent" a new and useful product.

Our system perfectly implements the stated purpose of the constitutional provision "to promote the progress of science" because, as James Madison explained in Federalist No. 43, it serves both the individual property rights and the public good. The U.S. patent system was unique when the

Founding Fathers wrote it into the Constitution, and it still is unique in the world today.

Many important inventors have attested that they would not have had the incentive to labor for years creating their invention were it not that our system offers hope that its profits will enable them to achieve the American dream. Our patent system, which protects the property right of the inventor, is why the United States has produced most of the world's great inventions and dominates the world in innovation. For more than two centuries, America's unique patent system has been the mainspring of our economic success.

All other countries award patents under an alien system called "first-to-file," i.e., the first person to file a paper with a government office. Foreign and powerful financial interests are now haranguing us to make us believe that the new dogma of globalism demands that we "harmonize" our patent system with the rest of the world by changing from first-to-invent to first-to-file.

A bill to do this (S.23) passed the Senate after a quickie hearing that did not include a single inventor, small business person, venture capital person, or constitutional authority. It's pushed without any publicity in the House as H.R.1249.

But harmonization makes no sense. Why would we abandon the proven best system that has worked successfully for more than two centuries and replace it with a proven inferior foreign system?

More important, this patent bill must be rejected because it is flat-out unconstitutional. The Constitution plainly states that the property right belongs to "inventors," not to someone handing a piece of paper to a government bureaucrat.

Seven scholarly law review articles have examined this issue and concluded that first-to-file is unconstitutional. No scholarly review proves otherwise.

We must not let Congress flout the Constitution by redefining the word "inventors" to be mean paper filers. The Constitution's framers, and the early Congresses (which included many men who had been members of the Constitutional Convention), were very clear that first-to-invent is the meaning of the word "inventors." First-to-invent is in conformity with tradition and history, as well as consistent with originalist, strict constructionist, and textualist views of the Constitution. More than two hundred years of statutes and jurisprudence confirm the first-to-invent standard.

The Patent Acts of 1790 and 1793 legislated that the patent must be awarded to "the first and true inventor." The Patent Act of 1836 used the language "original and true inventor" and "original and first inventor."

In Evans v. Jordan (1815), Chief Justice John Marshall wrote that the Constitution guarantees the "exclusive" right "to the inventor from the moment of invention." In Shaw v. Cooper (1833), the Supreme Court upheld the law that vested "the exclusive right in the inventor only."

The liberals are now circulating the un-American notion that we should utilize treaties and foreign laws to reinterpret our Constitution and statutes. They want Congress to use its Treaty power or its Commerce Clause power to override the inventors clause, overturn over 200 years of settled and successful law, and put us on the road to a borderless patent system.

First-to-file would elevate paperwork over true inventions, dilute the quality of patents because applications would be rushed to be filed, and cede sovereignty on the direction of our own patent system. First-to-file favors foreign inventors and big corporations that have the lawyers and resources to file quickly and redundantly, while taking rights away from independent inventors and small businesses.

No matter what arguments of policy or efficiency are made by first-to-file supporters, we cannot let them violate or ignore the Constitution. The unconstitutional patent bill should be defeated.

Dangerous to U.S. Security

More and more dangerous effects of the proposed changes to U.S. patent law (S.23, H.R.1249) keep emerging, especially since the hearings failed to hear from any real inventors. The proposed bill is not only unconstitutional; it is also an attack on our national security and an offense against the rule of law.

By awarding patents to the first-to-file an application with the bureaucracy instead of to the first-to-invent, the proposed bill will deprive inventors of their constitutional property right set forth in Article I, Section 8. U.S. law has always awarded patents to real inventors, not to paper-pushers.

An important letter sent to House Speaker John Boehner (R-OH) from the 15-member Inventors Network of the Capital Area describes how the proposed patent bill

165

"threatens all individual and corporate research & development in America, the backbone of our national defense and economic security." Here is how this racket will work.

The proposed patent bill will enable Chinese hackers to steal U.S. innovation secrets while they are still in development, then file an application with the U.S. Patent Office under first-to-file, and thereby own new U.S. technology instead of merely stealing it. Owning the patents will enable China legally to take away ownership rights and profits from Americans who actually invent new technologies.

Defense technologies would be a prime target of this threat. The first-to-file provision of the Patent Act would become the most effective weapon in China's arsenal and would threaten our national security in a new and ominously dangerous way.

National security expert Adam Segal testified before the House Foreign Affairs Subcommittee on Oversight and Investigations about the national security danger from Chinese cyber espionage, massive theft and piracy. Particularly dangerous is the Chinese policy called "indigenous innovation," which requires U.S. corporations to transfer their technology to China in order to get market access. He said, "it is clear that the United States must do more to defend itself."

Since 1870, U.S. law has provided a grace period of one year between the date the invention is disclosed and the date the patent application is submitted. This grace period gives an inventor a year to perfect his invention, to sort out better from inferior features, to raise capital, to gather partners, and to field test the invention before the deadline for filing a patent application.

This grace period is very important to independent inventors, small companies and startups. It permits them to delay the costs of filing until the invention is evaluated, a decision is made as to whether it is worth spending money on, and investment capital is raised.

Inventors don't usually give birth to their inventions like the Greek goddess Athena, who was born fully grown and fully armed out of Zeus's head. The Wright Brothers required many experiments as they tried wings with different angles before they were ready to patent heavier-than-air flight.

The proposed patent bill redefines the grace period in a way that is hostile to small inventors and small businesses because it states that any disclosure of the invention by anyone other than the inventor at any time, even within that first year, will bar the real inventor from getting a patent. Weakening the grace period thus poses an enormous risk to the most innovative sectors of our economy.

The value of first-to-invent plus grace period over first-to-file was explained by inventor Steve Perlman, CEO of Reardon, OnLive and MOVA. He experimented with 100 inventions over five years of development, but only six were actually used and filed for patents. He explained that a large part of invention is trying out a vast number of ideas, such as Edison with thousands of light bulb filaments and the Wright Brothers with many wing shapes. First-to-file means flooding the Patent Office with dead-end applications.

Another outrage of the proposed patent bill is the provision that subjects to expensive new litigation and retroactively attacks the patent on the check-clearing system which enables banks to return photo images to their depositors rather than actual canceled checks. This new system saves the banks millions of dollars because they no longer have to truck the checks physically to other banks to be cleared.

This system was created by inventor Claudio Ballard, who received a patent for it, survived post-grant review, and won expensive court battles when he defended his patent against infringement by the banks. After all that, the new patent bill (ignoring the principle of res judicata—the thing is already decided) sets up an unprecedented procedure to overturn the patent office and court decisions, giving the banks another chance to invalidate Ballard's patent.

A 15-page letter to Congress from Prof. Richard A. Epstein, the nation's foremost authority on property rights, explains how the "stacked procedures of Section 18" in the bill are designed to let banks use Ballard's invention without paying him for it. Epstein, who wrote the book on Takings under the Fifth Amendment, says Ballard deserves just compensation for the use of his patent. The Congressional Budget Office estimated that this "taking" of property rights could end up costing the taxpayers $1 billion.

Altogether, the proposed bill, mischievously called "patent reform," is a bad, dangerous and dishonest bill that must be defeated if we care about respecting the Constitution, inventors' property rights, and American leadership in innovation.

Now that the globalists have transferred millions of good American jobs to Asians willing to work for as little as 30 cents an hour with no benefits, all we have left to maintain and restore our economic wellbeing is our innovation superiority. The United States is the world leader in inventing useful and important products and processes, while other countries build their economies by copying our innovations.

Other countries are free to imitate our system, but foreign countries haven't copied our system. Instead, they want to copy our inventions, and they devise all sorts of tactics to cheat us. Their code word is harmonization; we are hammered with the agitprop that globalization requires us to harmonize our laws with the rest of the world (which does not include obligating foreigners to respect U.S. patents). It's a betrayal of American inventors to harmonize down to inferior foreign practices; let them harmonize up to our proven best system.

APPENDIX 1

An Open Letter to the
U.S. Senate by 25 Nobel Laureates
September 1997

We urge the Senate to oppose the passage of the
pending U.S. Senate Bill S.507 ... We believe that S.507 could
result in lasting harm to the United States and the world.

First, it will prove very damaging to American small
inventors and thereby discourage the flow of new inventions
that have contributed so much to America's superior
performance in the advancement of science and technology. It
will do so by curtailing the protection they obtain through
patents relative to the large multinational corporations.

Second, the principle of prior user rights saps the very
spirit of that wonderful institution that is represented by the
American patent system established in the Constitution in
1787, which is based on the principle that the inventor is given
complete protection but for a limited length of time, after
which the patent, fully disclosed in the application and
published at the time of issue, becomes in the public domain,

and can be used by anyone, under competitive conditions for the benefit of all final users.

Sidney Altman, (1989, Chemistry) Yale
Herbert C. Brown, (1979, Chemistry) Purdue
Robert F. Curl, (1996, Chemistry) Rice
Gertrude Elion, (1988, Medicine) Wellcome Research Labs
Jerome Friedman, (1990, Physics) MIT
Milton Friedman, (1976, Economics) University of Chicago
John C. Harsanyi, (1994, Economics) University of California at Berkeley
Herbert Hauptman, (1985, Chemistry) Hauptman-Woodward Medical Research Institute
Dudley Herschbach, (1986, Chemistry) Harvard
Roald Hoffman, (1981, Chemistry) Cornell
Henry Kendall, (1990, Physics) MIT
Har Gobind Khorana, (1968, Medicine) MIT
David M. Lee, (1996, Physics) Cornell
Merton Miller, (1990, Economics) University of Chicago
Franco Modigliani, (198 5, Economics) MIT
Mario Molina, (1995, Chemistry) MIT
Daniel Nathans, (1978, Medicine) Johns Hopkins
Douglass North, (1993, Economics) Washington University
Paul Samuelson, (1970, Economics) MIT
William Sharpe, (1990, Economics) Stanford
Clifford Shull, (1994, Physics) MIT
Herbert A. Simon, (1978, Economics) Carnegie-Mellon
Richard Smalley, (1996, Chemistry) Rice
Robert Solow, (1987, Economics) MIT
James Tobin, (1981, Economics) Yale

APPENDIX 2

No. 08-964

IN THE

Supreme Court of the United States

BERNARD L. BILSKI AND RAND A. WARSAW,

Petitioners,

v.

JOHN J. DOLL, ACTING UNDER SECRETARY OF COMMERCE FOR INTELLECTUAL PROPERTY AND ACTING DIRECTOR OF THE UNITED STATE PATENT AND TRADEMARK OFFICE,

Respondent.

BRIEF OF *AMICUS CURIAE* EAGLE FORUM EDUCATION & LEGAL DEFENSE IN SUPPORT OF PETITIONERS

ANDREW L. SCHLAFLY
Counsel for Amicus

QUESTIONS PRESENTED

Whether the Federal Circuit erred by holding that a "process" must be tied to a particular machine or apparatus, or transform a particular article into a different state or thing ("machine-or-transformation" test), to be eligible for patenting under 35 U.S.C. § 101, despite this Court's precedent declining to limit the broad statutory grant of patent eligibility for "any" new and useful process beyond excluding patents for "laws of nature, physical phenomena, and abstract ideas."

Whether the Federal Circuit's "machine-or-transformation" test for patent eligibility, which effectively forecloses meaningful patent protection to many business methods, contradicts the clear Congressional intent that patents protect "method[s] of doing or conducting business," 35 U.S.C. § 273.

INTEREST OF *AMICUS CURIAE*

Eagle Forum Education and Legal Defense Fund ("EFELDF"), a nonprofit organization founded in 1981, is a pro-family group that has long advocated fidelity to the text of the U.S. Constitution. EFELDF has a longstanding interest in defending rights of inventors and private property in general and has previously filed amicus briefs in federal courts on the issue of intellectual property. The mission of EFELDF includes defending the Patent Clause and the intellectual property rights of individual inventors, which are so crucial to American prosperity.

SUMMARY OF ARGUMENT

The Patent Clause is one of the most important provisions in the entire Constitution due to its central and essential role in promoting American ingenuity and prosperity. Though the Patent Clause receives scant historical attention—merely one paragraph addresses it in The Federalist No. 43—this unique American constitutional right has motivated the vast majority of the world's greatest inventions. From Thomas Edison to Alexander Graham Bell to many of today's greatest inventions, the Patent Clause has played an instrumental role in encouraging and protecting the individual's right to the fruits of his creative efforts. It must continue to do so no less in this Information Age.

The decision below usurps the legislative role and adds complexities to patent law that are neither welcome nor justified in the 21st century. If the invention at bar "promote[s] the Progress of Science and useful Arts," U.S. Const. Art. I, Sect. 8, Cl. 8, and if it satisfies the legislative requirements pursuant to that provision, then it is patentable subject matter. By adhering to the anachronistic "machine-or-transformation" test, which can be found in neither the Patent Clause nor its implementing statute, the court below improperly eviscerated much of the value of the patent system for the future. The incentives-based and natural rights-based approaches to intellectual property, which have always been the hallmark of the American patent system, should not be encumbered by outdated categorical exclusions based on machines and transformations.

The claim at bar is for a method of hedging commodities risk. Suppliers of goods would like to hedge their risk against a market drop in price; consumers of goods (such as manufacturers) would like to hedge their risk against a market increase in price. The patent claim describes use of an intermediary, called the "commodity provider," which would buy and sell at fixed prices as sought by the ultimate suppliers and consumers. The patent claim also extends beyond that to encompass the trading of options.

The patent examiner rejected these claims (1-11) under 35 U.S.C. § 101 because "the invention is not implemented on a specific apparatus and merely manipulates [an] abstract idea and solves a purely mathematical problem without any limitation to a practical application, therefore, the invention is not directed to the technological arts." In *re Bilski*, 545 F.3d 943, 950 (Fed. Cir. 2008). The Patent Board affirmed on different grounds, holding that transformation of "non-physical financial risks and legal liabilities of the commodity provider, the consumer, and the market participants" is not patentable subject matter. Id. (quotations omitted). The Board also noted that Applicants' claimed process did not produce a "useful, concrete and tangible result," and thus was not patentable subject matter. Id. (quotations omitted). The Federal Circuit affirmed, but on the grounds that the patent claim did not satisfy the "machine-or-transformation" test.

But Congress has not categorically excluded from patentability inventions that fail a "machine-or-transformation" test, and it was error for the lower court to impose that limitation. If an invention is obvious and thereby fails the "non-obvious" test, then a patent application for such invention may be rejected. Similarly, if an invention is outside the constitutional scope of the "Progress of Science and useful Arts," then Congress itself may not secure its protection under the Patent Clause. But the Federal Circuit erred in not deciding the patentability of the invention on either of those grounds, and instead grafting complex and unjustified requirements such as and especially the "machine-or-transformation" test. This test is unsuitable for the 21st century, it is inconsistent with the enormously successful incentives-based approach taken by the Framers, and it is contrary to a textualist interpretation of the applicable legislation and of the Patent Clause itself.

The separate dissents below by Judges Newman and Rader set valuable guideposts for reversal of the errant majority decision. Judge Newman correctly observed:

> The court thus excludes many of the kinds of inventions that apply today's electronic and photonic technologies, as well as other processes that handle data and information in novel ways. Such processes have long been patent eligible, and contribute to the vigor and variety of today's Information Age. This exclusion of process inventions is contrary to statute, contrary to precedent, and a negation of the constitutional mandate. Its impact on the future, as well as on the thousands of patents already granted, is unknown.

In *re Bilski*, 545 F.3d at 976 (Newman, J., dissenting).

Judge Rader aptly dissented on the grounds that the lower court had "ventured away from the statute":

[A]s innovators seek the path to the next techno-revolution, this court ties our patent system to dicta from an industrial age decades removed from the bleeding edge. A direct reading of the Supreme Court's principles and cases on patent eligibility would yield the one-sentence resolution suggested above. Because this court, however, links patent eligibility to the age of iron and steel at a time of subatomic particles and terabytes, I must respectfully dissent.

Id. at 1011 (Rader, J., dissenting). Judge Rader observed that "this court today invents several circuitous and unnecessary tests" and that other "statutory conditions and requirements better serve the function of screening out unpatentable inventions than some vague 'transformation' or 'proper machine link' test." *Id.* at 1015.

The applicable statute never mentions "transformations" and the decision below usurps the legislative role to impose the "machine-or-transformation" threshold test on patentability. Many valuable inventions that could propel the American economy will be lost if the judicial activism below is not reversed and the full rights of the individual inventor are not restored. This Court should then remand this case for a determination of whether the Bilski process is patentable under the statutory criteria set forth by Congress, not under a judicial test unsupported by precedent and without basis in the statute or the Patent Clause itself.

ARGUMENT

Three points are essential to deciding this appeal. First, continued vitality in the patent system for small inventors is essential to continued American prosperity. Second, a categorical exclusion from patentability of subject matter that lacks a "machine-or-transformation" is unjustified and ill-suited to inventions in the Information Age. Third, the much-lamented flaws in the current patent system are due to a lack of enforcement of other statutory requirements, such as the non-obviousness test. A judicial redefinition of the patent process is neither needed nor appropriate.

Categorical exclusion of patentable subject matter from 35 U.S.C. § 101 is misguided. As explained further below, *Amicus* EFELDF urges this Court to reexamine and adopt the reasoning set forth by Justice Potter Stewart in his dissent in *Parker v. Flook*:

[I]t strikes what seems to me an equally damaging blow at basic principles of patent law by importing into its inquiry under 35 U. S. C. § 101 the criteria of novelty and inventiveness. Section 101 is concerned only with subject-matter patentability. Whether a patent will actually *issue* depends upon the criteria of §§ 102 and 103, which include novelty and inventiveness, among many others. It may well be that under the criteria of §§ 102 and 103 no patent should issue on the process claimed in this case, because of anticipation, abandonment, obviousness, or for some other reason. But in my view the claimed process clearly meets the standards of subject-matter patentability of § 101.

437 U.S. 584, 600 (1978) (Stewart, J., dissenting)

I. THE FEDERAL CIRCUIT ERRED IN HOLDING THAT A PROCESS MUST ALWAYS BE TIED TO A PARTICULAR MACHINE OR APPARATUS TO BE PATENTABLE

The central error in the decision below was its categorical denial of the patent application based on the "machine-or-transformation test," which the Court described as follows:

The machine-or-transformation test is a two-branched inquiry; an applicant may show that a process claim satisfies § 101 either by showing that his claim is tied to a particular machine, or by showing that his claim transforms an article. *See Benson*, 409 U.S. at 70. Certain considerations are applicable to analysis under either branch. First, as illustrated by *Benson* and discussed below, the use of a specific machine or transformation of an article must impose meaningful limits on the claim's scope to impart patent-eligibility. *See Benson*, 409 U.S. at 71-72. Second, the involvement of the machine or transformation in the claimed process must not merely be insignificant extra-solution activity. *See Flook*, 437 U.S. at 590.

In *re Bilski*, 545 F.3d 943, 963 (Fed. Cir. 2008) (emphasis added).

The decision below held as a threshold matter that "the operative question ... is whether Applicants' claim 1 satisfies the transformation branch of the machine-or-transformation test." The Court held that it does not:

We hold that the Applicants' process as claimed does not transform any article to a different state or thing. Purported transformations or manipulations simply of public or private legal obligations or relationships, business risks, or other such abstractions cannot meet the test because they are not physical objects or substances, and they are not representative of physical objects or substances. Applicants' process at most incorporates only such ineligible transformations. ... [C]laim 1 does not involve the transformation of any physical object or substance, or an electronic signal representative of any physical object or substance. **Given its admitted failure to meet the machine implementation part of the test as well, the claim entirely fails the machine-or-transformation test and is not drawn to patent-eligible subject matter.**

Id. at 963 (emphasis added).

This categorical exclusion from patentability unwisely and unjustifiably excludes desirable innovations from the protection of patent law. For example, Samuel Morse obtained a patent for the following claim for his Morse Code:

> Fifth, I claim, as my invention, the system of signs, consisting of dots and spaces, and of dots, spaces, and horizontal lines, for numerals, letters, words or sentences, substantially as herein set forth and illustrated, for telegraphic purposes.

O'Reilly v. Morse, 56 U.S. 62, 1853 U.S. LEXIS 273, *49 (1854). It seems doubtful that this claim would survive the machine-or-transformation test imposed by the decision below. Part of the enormous value of Morse Code is that it is machine *independent*.

Many great inventions of the Information Age are valuable precisely *because of their machine independence*, such as the UNIX operating system and the "MP3" music player format. The essence of the real breakthrough of these inventions is their independence of particular machines. Copyright law protects the software program code itself, but the true invention (what the code does) is not adequately protected by copyrights on the code.

It is unwise and unjustified to categorically exclude from patentability anything and everything that is decoupled from a physical process. For the UNIX operating system, the invention's value was the lack of a link to a specific computer machine and the fact that it is not hooked to any particular (physical) hardware. The decision below will not properly incentivize future inventions like UNIX, and even more abstract yet extremely valuable and desirable ones, if the anachronistic "machine-or-transformation" test is affirmed here. Patent law should not be limited by arbitrary physicality, but should be able to look more to the utility of the novel work.

This machine-or-transformation test imposed below also creates more questions than it answers. It leaves unclear what link to a machine is adequate, an issue of particular importance for the vast number of computer-related inventions. As pointed out by Judge Rader in dissent:

What link to a machine is sufficient to invoke the "or machine" prong? Are the "specific" machines of *Benson* required, or can a general purpose computer qualify? What constitutes "extra-solution activity?" If a process may meet eligibility muster as a "machine," why does the Act "require" a machine link for a "process" to show eligibility? Does the rule against redundancy itself suggest an inadequacy in this complex spider web of tests supposedly "required" by the language of section 101?

In re Bilski, 545 F.3d at 1015 (Rader, J., dissenting).

This lower court's "machine-or-transformation" requirement is harmful in several ways. It will suppress and discourage invention—and thereby prosperity—in a way that the Constitution does not support and that Congress has not authorized. This unjustified requirement is also difficult to implement and enforce. As Judge Rader noted in dissent below, this test strays from a straightforward, textualist reading of the applicable statute, and instead reads a whole new test into the statute that was never in-tended.

II. THE UNDERLYING FLAW IN THE CURRENT PATENT PROCESS IS LACK OF ENFORCEMENT OF OTHER STATUTORY PROVISIONS, WHICH HURTS INNOVATION

As Justice Potter Stewart wrote in his dissent in *Parker v. Flook*, "[w]hether a patent will actually issue depends upon the criteria of §§ 102 and 103, which include novelty and inventiveness, among many others." 437 U.S. 584, 600 (1978) (Stewart, J., dissenting). It is a lack of enforcement of the novelty and inventiveness requirements that causes the underlying flaws in the current patent process.

Copyright law, by analogy, has successfully adhered to its originality requirement to help keep out non-meritorious claims. This

Court held without dissent that "[o]riginality is a constitutional requirement." *Feist Publ'ns, Inc. v. Rural Tel. Serv. Co.*, 499 U.S. 340, 346 (1991). "The originality requirement articulated in *The Trade-Mark Cases* and *Burrow-Giles* remains the touchstone of copyright protection today. It is the very premise of copyright law." *Id.* at 347 (quotations and citations omitted).

Similarly, the better approach to curb abuses in patent law is to strengthen the requirement of originality rather than erect complex, non-statutory obstacles to patentability. As Judge Newman explained in his dissent, the lower court's "exclusion is imposed at the threshold, before it is determined whether the excluded process is new, non-obvious, enabled, described, particularly claimed, etc.; that is, before the new process is examined for patentability." *In re Bilski*, 545 F.3d at 976 (Newman, J., dissenting).

Other "statutory conditions and requirements better serve the function of screening out unpatentable inventions than some vague 'transformation' or 'proper machine link' test." *Id.* at 1015 (Rader, J., dissenting).

This Court should affirm the approach taken by Judge Rader below:

> If this court would follow that Supreme Court rule, it would afford broad patent protection to new and useful inventions that fall within the enumerated categories and satisfy the other conditions of patentability. **That is, after all, precisely what the statute says.**

In re Bilski, 545 F.3d at 1011·12 (Rader, J., dissenting) (emphasis added).

III. ROBUST PATENT LAW THAT PROTECTS SMALL INVENTORS IS ESSENTIAL TO CONTINUED AMERICAN PROSPERITY

"Patents provide an incentive to invest in and work in new directions," observed Judge Newman in dissent below. *In re Bilski*,

545 F.3d at 997 (Newman, J., dissenting). Those incentives are essential to continued American prosperity.

The Patent Clause and its statutory implementation inspired some of the greatest inventions in the history of mankind. Thomas Edison, properly recognized as the most influential person in the world during the entire second millennium by *Life* magazine, was motivated by the patent system to obtain 1,093 patents in the United States. The patent system provided enormous incentives for Edison for his ingenuity, and as a result the entire world reaped prodigious rewards. Without the full and robust protections of patent law, ingenuity by the small inventor is diminished and the American economy suffers from a lack of incentives for valuable inventions. The anachronistic "machine-or-transformation" test forecloses the future Thomas Edisons of the Information Age. A marvelous new invention that fails the "machine-or-transformation" test may still be something that we want to encourage. The "machine-or-transformation" is simply too rigid to adapt to changing times. The future equivalent of the light bulb or power station might well be intangible and thereby fail the overly-restrictive "machine-or-transformation" test.

As in the analogous field of copyright law, "It is generally for Congress, not the courts, to decide how best to pursue the Copyright Clause's objectives." *Eldred v. Ashcroft*, 537 U.S. 186, 212 (2003). This aphorism applies with even greater force to the Patent Clause. Patents play an even more vital role in protecting and encouraging ingenuity and productivity. The wooden "machine-or-transformation" test imposed below will inevitably stifle inventions and innovation. Courts should not meddle with the important incentives for invention created by Congress based on the Patent Clause.

As Justice Burton, joined by Chief Justice Vinson and Justice Frankfurter, observed over a half-century ago:

> the frontiers of science have expanded until civilization now depends largely upon discoveries on those frontiers to meet the infinite needs of the future. The United States, thus far,

has taken a leading part in making those discoveries and in putting them to use.

United States v. Line Material Co., 333 U.S. 287, 332 (1948) (Burton, J., dissenting). Patentability should not be locked into the anachronisms of the past, and incentives for original inventions for the future must be fully preserved.

CONCLUSION

The decision below should be reversed.

Respectfully submitted,

ANDREW L. SCHLAFLY
Counsel for Amicus

Dated: August 6, 2009

APPENDIX 3

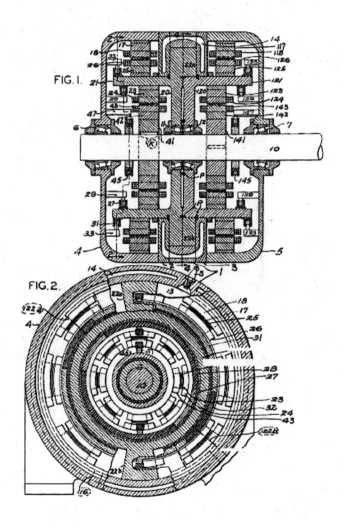

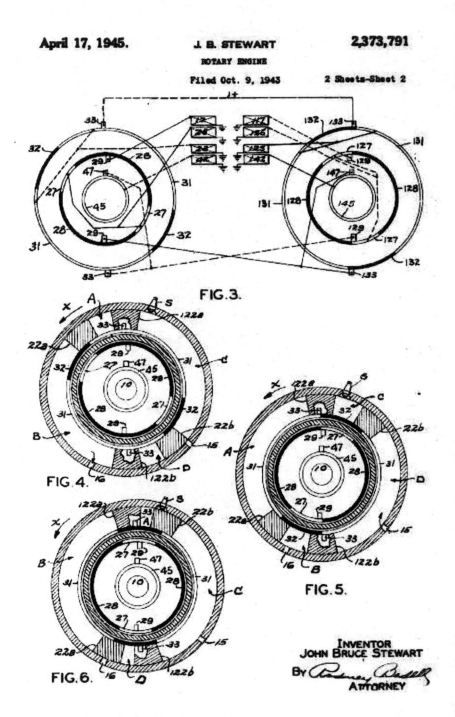

April 17, 1945.

J. B. STEWART

2,373,791

ROTARY ENGINE

Filed Oct. 9, 1943

2 Sheets-Sheet 2

FIG. 3.

FIG. 4.

FIG. 5.

FIG. 6.

INVENTOR
JOHN BRUCE STEWART
By
ATTORNEY

Patented Apr. 17, 1945
2,373,791

UNITED STATES PATENT OFFICE
2,373,791
ROTARY ENGINE
John Bruce Stewart, St. Louis, Mo.
Application October 9, 1943, Serial No. 505,627
21 Claims (Cl. 123-11)

The invention relates to engines involving relatively movable rotors in a circular cylinder structure whereby fluid alternately compressed and expanded between the rotors serves to drive a power shaft or whereby a driven power shaft drives the rotors to draw in and discharge fluid between them. The invention may be embodied, for example, in an internal combustion engine, in a steam or compressed air engine, or in a compressor or pump for air, water or other fluid.

One object of the invention is to provide a rotary engine of the type described of relatively few parts, all rotating in the same direction and in themselves producing desired absolute pressures on fluids in the cylinder structure and coacting so as to render the engine effective, particularly at high speeds.

Another object is to provide a rotary engine of the type described free of ratchets and pawls and free of spring actuated parts, thereby reducing expense of construction and maintenance and wear incident to wear and replacement of such parts.

A more specific object of the invention is to transfer momentum from one moving rotor to another moving rotor, thus reducing or eliminating the loss of energy resulting in rotary engines in which one rotor is brought to a stop before the other rotor begins to move.

Rotary engines may comprise means for successively and alternately locking the rotors to the cylinder and shaft respectively. Another object is to effect in such engines the locking of the rotors to the cylinder and shaft respectively through cushioned means, thereby freeing the mechanism of repeated shocks from abrupt stopping of the rotors. This object may be obtained by using magnetism for locking the rotors to the cylinder and shaft respectively, and it is another object to utilize electromagnets controlled by the rotation of the engine parts to secure the rotors to the shaft and frame respectively intermittently for effecting a continuous delivery of power by the engine.

Another object is to balance the parts and their power impulses so as to provide for smooth operation of the engine.

These and other detail objects of the invention are attained by the structure shown in the accompanying drawings in which—

Figure 1 is a section taken through an internal combustion rotary engine on a plane extending longitudinally of its axis.

Figure 2 is a transverse section taken on the line 2-2 of Figure 1.

Figure 3 is a wiring diagram of the electromagnetic circuits.

Figure 4 is a transverse section taken on the line 4-4 of Figure 1 but largely diagrammatic and drawn to a smaller scale and showing the rotor pistons in the positions assumed at one point in the cycle of operations and also indicating the positions of the magnet circuit controls on one rotor.

Figures 5 and 6 correspond to Figure 4 but illustrate the parts in successive positions assumed during the cycle of operation of the engine.

The engine frame is built up and comprises a central ring 1, side plates 2 and 3 and end bells or housings 4 and 5. Ring 1 and plates 2 and 3 form a continuous inwardly facing peripheral cylinder 13. A substantially continuous water jacket 14 extends around three sides of cylinder 13 and cooling water is circulated through this water jacket in any well known manner. A port 15 (Figures 2, 4-6) provides for the intake of fuel to cylinder 13 and a port 16 provides for the exhaust of the products of combustion from the cylinder.

Antifriction bearing units 6 and 7 are mounted in housings 4 and 5 respectively and journal a shaft 10 which in turn carries antifriction bearing units 11 and 12 which journal rotors 20 and 120 respectively, each having an annular rim **21** and **121** respectively, extending parallel to the shaft, and each rotor has a pair of radially extending pistons **22a**, **22b** and **122a**, **122b** respectively received in cylinder 13 and corresponding in cross section to the cross section of the cylinder. The inner open side of the cylinder between successive pistons is closed by the periphery of rotor rims **21** and **121**. Suitable packing elements P are provided to seal the joints between the cylinder and rotors.

As so far described, the two rotors and shaft are rotatable relative to each other and to the frame which may be assumed as remaining stationary. The following structure provides means for securing the rotors to the shaft and to the frame intermittently. In the operation, each rotor is secured to the shaft and to the frame alternately and while one rotor is secured to the shaft the other rotor is secured to the frame. The means securing the rotors as mentioned comprises a series of devices utilizing magnetism controlled by electric circuits which, in turn, are opened and closed by the rotation of the rotors about the shaft axis. The term "secured" is intended to express the relation existing between mutually attracted parts although during a portion of each "securing" period there will be relative movement of those parts prior to the synchronizing or unitary action of those parts.

Structurally the securing means for each rotor may be considered independent of the securing means for the other rotor and the securing means for rotor **20** will be described in detail, it being understood that these means are duplicated for rotor **120** and that the same reference numerals with the hundreds digit added apply to the parts on rotor **120**. A collar **41** is keyed to shaft **10** at K and on its external surface is fixed a series of electromagnets comprising successive cores **42** having coils **43** wound in opposite directions about successive cores forming the alternating north and south magnetic poles.

A series of cooperating magnets is fixed upon the inner periphery of rotor rim **21**. The cores or poles of these magnets are indicated at **23** and their windings at **24**.

A corresponding series of magnets is fixed upon the outer periphery of rotor rim **21** and the cores of these magnets are indicated at **25** and their windings at **26**. Cooperating magnets are fixed on the inner periphery of housing **4** and the cores of these magnets are indicated at **17** and their windings at **18**.

Mounted on shaft **10** is a collector ring **45** having a continuous circuit forming periphery. A stationary brush **41** on housing **4** engages ring **45**.

A ring mounted on the inner periphery of rotor rim **21** comprises two circuit forming segments **27** diametrically opposite each other and each extending approximately 43° and alternating with insulation segments **28**, each extending approximately 137°. Stationary brushes **29** on housing **4** engage segments **27** and **28**.

A ring mounted on the exterior periphery of rotor rim **21** comprises two circuit forming segments **31** each extending approximately 137° and alternating with insulation segments **32** each extending approximately 43°. Stationary brushes **33** on housing **4** engage segments **31** and **32**.

The wiring diagram (Figure 3, showing the rings in the position indicated in Figure 4) indicates that the windings of frame magnets **17** and cooperating outer magnets **25** on rotor **20** are in the same circuit as the windings of shaft magnets **142** and cooperating inner magnets **123** on rotor **120** and, conversely, that frame magnets **117** and cooperating outer magnets **125** on rotor **120** are in the same circuit as shaft magnets **42** and cooperating inner magnets **23** on rotor **20**. Hence, when one rotor is secured to the frame, the other rotor will be secured to the shaft and vice versa.

Operation—With the above structural description in mind, the operation of the engine should be readily understood by reference to the following description of critical successive positions of the rotors, reference being had to Figures 4-6, it being understood that the rotors are turning in an anticlockwise direction as indicated by the arrow X. Magnets **117** and **125** are energized and rotor **120** may be considered stationary. Magnets **23** and **42** are also energized and are securing rotor **20** to the shaft. The fuel charge in chamber A between piston **122a** and piston **22a** has been ignited and is expanding, delivering a driving impulse to piston **22a** and accelerating the movement of the same and rotor **20** and the shaft. Gas in chamber B between the forward side of piston **22a** and the rear face of piston **122b** on rotor **120** is being exhausted through exhaust port **16** and another charge of fuel in chamber C between the rear face of piston **122a** and the forward face of piston **22b** is being compressed and as soon as piston **22b** passes intake port **15**, another charge of fuel is drawn through the intake port into chamber D between the rear face of piston **22b** and the forward face of piston **122b**. (See Figure 5.)

When the parts reach the position shown in Figure 5, the driving impulse from the ignited expanding fuel will have been absorbed and further rotation of the shaft and rotor **20** as a unit would cause the rotor to exert a drag upon the shaft. At this point, however, insulation segments **32** interrupt the current to magnets **23** and **42**, deenergizing the same and leaving shaft **10** and rotor **20** free to rotate independently of each other. The momentum of piston **22b** causes it to further compress the charge in chamber C. At the same time, insulation segments **32** and **128** interrupt the current to magnets **117** and **125** holding rotor **120** to the frame, deenergizing the same, and rotor **120** is free to move under the thrust exerted upon the rear face of its piston **122a** by the compressed fuel charge in chamber C. Also collector segments **131** contact their brushes and magnets **123** and **142** are energized, whereby rotor **120** is attracted to the shaft just as rotor **20** was secured at the beginning of the operation being described. As rotor **20** decelerates and rotor **120** accelerates, the piston **22b** approaches piston **122a** more closely than at any other point in the cycle (see Figure 6) and just prior to the instant of their closest approach, rotor **20** closes the circuit for the spark plug S, igniting the charge and subjecting piston **122a** and rotor **120** to a driving impulse corresponding to that just described for rotor **20**. Thereupon piston **22b** assumes the position occupied by piston **122a** in Figure 4, rotor **20** is locked to the frame and rotor **120** and its pistons exhaust the gas from the previous explosion, compress the fuel charge for the next explosion and draw in the fuel charge for the following explosion.

During the movement of the rotors from the position shown in Figure 5 to the position shown in Figure 6; the momentum of the rapidly moving rotor **20** is being delivered to the more slowly moving rotor **120** and the movement of rotor **20** will be substantially three times the movement of rotor **120**. When the rotors reach the relative position shown in Figure 6, the speed of the two rotors is approximately equal. During the movement of rotor **20** from the position shown in Figure 6 to the position in which its piston **22b** is upright, corresponding to the position of piston **122a** in Figure 4, the movement of rotor **120** is substantially three times as great as that of rotor **20**.

From this description, it will be seen that the impulse applied to a rotor by the explosion of the fuel charge is transmitted to the shaft but, when the force of the expanding fuel charge is substantially exhausted and it becomes necessary to free the shaft and rotor so as to avoid the rotor acting as a drag on the shaft, the momentum of the rotor, although not so great as that of the shaft, is not dissipated but is transferred to the previously stationary rotor (which is now released from the frame) and serves to give the latter rotor a start on its impulse-receiving movement so that by the time the expansion of the ignited fuel becomes effective the latter rotor is substantially synchronized with the shaft and is locked thereto and may deliver to the shaft the substantially full impulse from the expanded fuel. The transfer of momentum from one rotor to the other not only avoids waste of energy but also brings the decelerating rotor to a stop easily and avoids shocks which otherwise would be sustained if the movement of the decelerating rotor were arrested by mechanical means as distinguished from the elastic magnetic means.

Each time a rotor is subjected to the attraction of a different group of magnets, there will be a position just prior to the end of its deceleration or acceleration, as the case may be, when the south poles of the cooperating magnets will be opposed and the north poles of the cooperating magnets will be opposed. This will expedite the final movement of the rotor into its temporary locked position, i.e. stationary with the frame or synchronized with the shaft.

192

It will be understood that under the conditions described the movements of the rotors tend to become continuous and the velocity of the shaft will increase to a point determined by the fuel charge and the capacity of the engine, when the velocity will continue substantially uniform under a given load.

Obviously, the number of moving parts is minimized and these parts are of simple construction and free of cams, pins, wedges, stop blocks, springs, etc. as have characterized rotary engines of the same general type.

It will be understood that the brushes will be mounted so as to be moved angularly about the shaft for a short distance to effect the best timing of the shifting of the magnetic circuits relative to the igniting of the fuel charge. Obviously the relative lengths of the collecting and insulation segments of the rings may be varied to secure desired results.

While the above description relates particularly to an internal combustion engine, it will be understood that the novel features described are adapted for use in a steam or compressed air engine or a Diesel type engine. Also, by positively actuating the shaft from an external source, the structure may be utilized as a pump or compressor and, instead of the fluid drawn in between the successive pistons furnishing a power impulse, such fluid will be delivered from the cylinder under pressure.

Other details of the structure may be modified substantially in other ways than indicated without departing from the spirit of the invention and the exclusive use of those modifications coming within the scope of the claims is contemplated.

What is claimed is:

1. In a rotary engine, a shaft member, a circular cylinder member surrounding the same, relatively movable pistons in the cylinder member, means temporarily locking the pistons to the shaft member and to the cylinder member respectively and alternately, the means for locking the pistons to at least one of the members comprising a periodically energized and deenergized electromagnet.

2. In a rotary engine, a shaft member, a circular cylinder surrounding the same, relatively movable pistons in the cylinder,

periodically energized and deenergized electromagnetic means for temporarily locking the pistons to the power shaft and to the cylinder respectively and alternately.

3. In a rotary engine, a shaft member, a circular cylinder member surrounding the same, relatively movable pistons in the cylinder member, means temporarily locking the pistons to the shaft member and to the cylinder member respectively and alternately, the means for locking the pistons to at least one of the members comprising an electromagnet the circuit of which is closed and opened by the movement of the pistons to a predetermined angular position about the shaft and cylinder.

4. In a rotary internal combustion engine, a power shaft, a circular cylinder surrounding the same, relatively movable pistons therein, magnetic means for temporarily locking respective pistons to the shaft and cylinder, a fuel inlet to the cylinder between said pistons, and means for igniting the fuel controlled by the positioning of one of the pistons irrespective of the angular position of the shaft.

5. In a rotary internal combustion engine, a power shaft, a circular cylinder surrounding the same, relatively movable pistons therein, magnetic means for successively locking and releasing the pistons to the shaft and to the cylinder respectively and alternately, a fuel inlet port leading to the cylinder between the pistons, and a fuel ignition system, said port and ignition system being controlled by the positioning of the piston irrespective of the angular position of said shaft.

6. In a rotary internal combustion engine, a power shaft, a circular cylinder surrounding the same, two pistons movable separately in the cylinder, electromagnetic devices successively looking each of the pistons to the power shaft and to the cylinder respectively and alternately, a fuel inlet to said cylinder whereby a charge of fuel may be drawn into the cylinder between two pistons during their relative movement away from each other, means for igniting the charge, and timing means controlling said devices and effecting release of the piston locked to the power shaft prior to the

release of the piston locked to the cylinder and effecting release of the latter mentioned piston prior to the ignition of the fuel charge.

7. In a rotary internal combustion-engine, a power shaft, a circular cylinder surrounding the same, two pistons movable separately in the cylinder, electromagnetic devices successively locking each of the pistons to the power shaft and to the cylinder respectively and alternately, a port for admitting fuel to a space between the pistons during a portion of their relative movement away from each other when adjacent the port, means for igniting the charge, and timing means controlling said devices and effecting release of the piston locked to the power shaft prior to the release of the piston locked to the cylinder and effecting release of the latter-mentioned piston prior to the ignition of the fuel charge.

8. In an internal combustion rotary engine, a power shaft, a circular cylinder surrounding the same, a forward piston and a rear piston in the cylinder, electromagnetic devices temporarily locking the forward piston to the cylinder and the rear piston to the shaft during a portion of the cycle of operation, a fuel intake to the cylinder between the pistons when so locked and spaced substantially from the forward piston, a fuel ignition system, magnet-current-controlling means for releasing the rear piston from the shaft after it passes the intake and as the compression of the fuel between the pistons reaches the desired pressure, and means for releasing the forward piston from the cylinder before said compression stops the rear piston so that momentum of the rear piston will be transferred to the forward piston through the compressed fuel and prior to ignition of the fuel.

9. An engine as described in claim 8 which includes electromagnetic means locking the forward piston to the shaft and locking the rear piston to the cylinder after the forward piston has received momentum from the rear piston, the ignition being synchronized with the latter mentioned means to cause combustion of the fuel to propel the forward piston after the latter mentioned locking has occurred.

10. In an internal combustion rotary engine, a power shaft, a circular cylinder surrounding the same, four pistons movable therein

and arranged in pairs, the pistons of each pair being spaced apart but rigid with each other, periodically energized electromagnetic means for locking each pair of pistons to the cylinder and shaft alternately, a fuel intake, a fuel exhaust, an ignition system and timing means controlling said locking means so that the pistons are locked simultaneously to the cylinder and shaft alternately once during each rotation of the shaft and the intake and exhaust and ignition system function twice during each rotation of the shaft.

11. In an internal combustion rotary engine, a power shaft, a circular cylinder surrounding the same, a pair of pistons movable relative to each other in the cylinder, a fuel intake to the cylinder, a fuel exhaust from the cylinder, an igniter for fuel in the cylinder, and electromagnetic means for locking the pistons to the cylinder and shaft respectively and alternately at predetermined points in the movement of the pistons through the cylinder, and means controlled by the positions of the pistons so that rotation of the pistons by the ignition of the fuel charge; and its subsequent expansion effects compression of the ensuing fuel charge and continued rotation of the shaft and discharge of the burnt fuel.

12. In an internal combustion rotary engine, a power shaft, a circular cylinder surrounding the same, a pair of pistons in the cylinder, electromagnetic means for locking the pistons individually to the cylinder and shaft alternately, timing means controlling the electromagnetic circuit so that the rear piston is locked to the shaft and moves towards the forward piston while the latter is locked to the cylinder and forms a part thereof, a fuel intake to the cylinder between the pistons and spaced substantially from the forward piston when it is looked as described, the timing means causing said electromagnetic circuit to release the rear piston from the shaft as the compression in the cylinder between the pistons reaches the desired pressure and causing the electromagnetic circuit to release the forward piston from the cylinder before said compression stops the rear piston so that the forward piston will receive the momentum of the rear piston, and causing the electromagnetic circuit to lock the rear piston to the cylinder and the forward piston to the shaft as the momentum of the two pistons approaches equalization, and means

for igniting the charge synchronously with the latter-mentioned locking of the pistons to the cylinder and shaft respectively, said timing means effecting energization of the electromagnetic circuit during the approach of the pistons to their locking positions, whereby the electromagnetic circuit contributes to the movement of the pistons through the cylinder.

13. In an internal combustion rotary engine, a power shaft, a circular cylinder surrounding the same, a pair of pistons in the cylinder, electromagnetic means for locking the pistons individually to the cylinder and shaft alternately, timing devices controlling said means so that a piston may be locked to the shaft and moved towards another piston while the latter is locked to the stationary cylinder and forms a part thereof, a fuel-intake to the cylinder between the pistons and spaced substantially from the forward piston when it is locked as described, the timing devices causing said means to release the rear piston from the shaft as the compression in the cylinder between the pistons reaches the desired pressure, and causing said means to release the forward piston from the cylinder before the rear piston is locked to the cylinder so that the forward piston will receive momentum of the rear piston, and causing said means to lock the rear piston to the cylinder and the forward piston to the shaft as the momentum of the two pistons approaches equalization, and means for igniting the charge synchronously with the latter-mentioned locking of the pistons to the cylinder and shaft respectively.

14. In a rotary internal combustion engine, a power shaft, a pair of rotors thereon, a piston on each rotor, a stationary frame including a circular cylinder surrounding the shaft and receiving the pistons, individual electromagnets for locking the rotors to the cylinder and to the power shaft selectively, the piston on the shaft-locked rotor moving towards the piston on the cylinder-locked rotor during a portion of the engine cycle to compress a fuel charge between the pistons, collector rings on the rotors and shaft, brushes on the frame associated with said rings, each ring having alternate conducting and insulating segments arranged about the axis of the rotors and shaft, the conducting segments being electrically connected to said magnets and the segments of the collector rings of

one rotor being staggered in part circumferentially of the shaft with the conducting segments of the collector rings of the other, rotor so that one rotor is locked to the shaft during the time that the other rotor is locked to the cylinder and the electromagnets locking one rotor to the shaft are energized as the compression in the cylinder reaches the desired pressure and the electromagnets holding the other rotor to the cylinder are deenergized before said compression stops the rear piston, whereby the forward piston will receive the momentum or velocity of the rear piston, and the electromagnet locking the forward piston to the power shaft and the rear piston to the cylinder will be energized as the momentum or velocity of the two pistons, and their rotors, is equalized, there being means for igniting the fuel charge when the desired compression is attained.

15. In a rotary engine, a power shaft, a pair of rotors thereon, pistons on each rotor, a circular cylinder surrounding the shaft and receiving the pistons, magnetic means for temporarily securing individual pistons to the shaft and cylinder respectively, ports for admitting fluid to the cylinder and for exhausting fluid from the cylinder, the charging and compression of, the fluid being effected by relative movement of the rotors and their pistons, the momentum of the more rapidly moving rotor being transferred to the other rotor through the admitted fluid compressed between the pistons and by the expansion of the fluid when ignited, and the momentum of the more rapidly moving rotor being transferred to the power shaft.

16. An engine as described in claim 15 in which the magnetic means effect in part the relative movement of the rotors.

17. In an engine, a shaft, a circular cylinder surrounding the same, rotors on said shaft with individual pistons in said cylinder, said rotors being movable relative to the shaft, the cylinder and each other, electromagnetic devices intermittently securing the rotors to the cylinder and shaft respectively, there being an inlet and an outlet to said cylinder, and means controlling the circuits for said devices and correlated with said rotors so that the relative movement of the rotors due to the intermittent securing of the same to the shaft and to the cylinder causes the space between their respective pistons to be subjected alternately to subatmospheric pressure and to super-

atmospheric pressure to draw fluid through said inlet into said cylinder and to exhaust fluid from the cylinder through said outlet.

18. An engine as described in claim 17 which includes means for igniting the fluid in the cylinder when it is subjected to superatmospheric pressure while one of the rotors is secured to the cylinder and the other rotor is secured to the shaft whereby the latter-mentioned rotor and the shaft are propelled by the expansion of the fluid.

19. In an internal combustion rotary engine, a power shaft, a circular cylinder surrounding the magnetic means for locking the pistons individually to the cylinder and shaft alternately, timing means controlling the electromagnetic circuit so that the rear piston is locked to the shaft and moves towards the forward piston while the latter is locked to the cylinder and forms a part thereof, a fuel intake to the cylinder between the pistons and spaced substantially from the forward piston when it is locked as described, the timing means causing said electromagnetic circuit to release the rear piston from the shaft as the compression in the cylinder between the pistons reaches the desired pressure and causing the electromagnetic circuit to release the forward piston from the cylinder before said compression stops the rear piston so that the forward piston will receive the momentum of the rear piston, and causing the electromagnetic circuit to lock the rear piston to the cylinder and the forward piston to the shaft as the momentum of the two pistons approaches equalization, and means for igniting the charge synchronously with the latter-mentioned locking of the pistons to the cylinder and shaft respectively.

20. In a rotary engine, a power shaft, a pair of rotors thereon, pistons on each rotor, a circular cylinder surrounding the shaft and receiving the pistons, a port for admitting fluid to the cylinder between the piston of one rotor and a piston of the other rotor, a port for exhausting fluid from the cylinder between the other pistons of the rotors, the momentum of the more rapidly moving rotor being transferred to the other rotor through the fluid between the two first-mentioned pistons, and electromagnetic means supplementing the action of the fluid pressure on the more slowly moving piston.

21. In a pump, a circular housing, a shaft disposed axially of the housing, pistons movable in the housing about said axis and relative to each other, electromagnetic devices intermittently securing each piston to the housing and to the shaft respectively, there being an inlet and an outlet to said housing, and means controlling the circuits for said devices and correlated with said pistons so that the relative movement of the pistons due to the intermittent securing of the same to the shaft and to the housing causes the space between successive pistons to be subjected alternately to subatmospheric pressure and to super-atmospheric pressure to draw fluid through said inlet into the housing and to exhaust fluid from the housing through said outlet.

JOHN BRUCE STEWART.

About Phyllis Schlafly

Phyllis Schlafly, nee Stewart, was politically active and became a leader of the conservative wing of the Republican Party and played a large role in creating the modern American Conservative Movement. She became a strong advocate for the American patent system and for inventors.

Her father, John Bruce Stewart, an inventor and patent owner, was unemployed during the Depression after being laid off by Westinghouse. He was issued a patent on a rotary engine after 17 years of working on it in his spare time. (See Appendix 2) One of Phyllis's sons, Roger, is a mathematician, inventor, patent owner, and patent agent.

Though Mr. Stewart's patent was not commercialized, Mazda and others outside the US have made the rotary engine a success. The patent was issued to Stewart during World War II. At that time, car makers probably were not interested in new kinds of engines as mass production was a priority. Also, as we know from the Tucker inventor saga, Detroit resisted new kinds of car engines and designs.

Phyllis's focus on invention, as part of the free enterprise system, showed throughout the stages of her career. In her book *The Power of the Positive Woman*, for instance, she named labor-saving inventions and extolled the inventors as "the real liberators of women in America." Phyllis was further influenced by her service on the Commission on the Bicentennial of the Constitution in the 1980s. Her work there crystalized her view of the Founders' approach on this property right and patents as a means to national wealth creation. She illustrated the constitutional point of Article I Section 8's patents clause with examples of disruptive inventions in numerous economic sectors, which both advanced the state of the art and improved the American standard of living (the light bulb, the telephone, the cotton gin, the sewing machine, etc.).

Phyllis engaged through her Eagle Forum educational and grassroots organization protecting and defending the unique American patent system that had given rise to iconic inventors, leapfrogging technology and economic growth as politicians and powerful interests sought to "harmonize" our patent system with those of foreign nations.

About Ed Martin

On September 28, 2015, Phyllis Schlafly named Ed Martin as her hand-picked successor. Ed had been working as a special assistant to Phyllis for more than two years. A lawyer and bioethicist by training, Ed had previously served as chairman of the Missouri Republican Party and chief of staff to Missouri Governor Matt Blunt. Ed lives in St. Louis, Missouri, with his wife and four children.